NOT TO SPEAK OF THE DOG
101 Short Stories in Verse

edited by
CHRISTOPHER REID

ff

faber and faber

First published in 2000
by Faber and Faber Limited
3 Queen Square London WC1N 3AU

Photoset by Wilmaset Ltd, Wirral
Printed in England by Clays Ltd, St Ives plc

A CIP record for this book
is available from the British Library
ISBN 0-571-20552-6

2 4 6 8 10 9 7 5 3 1

Contents

Introduction

This is not an orthodox collection of narrative verse. What will be immediately obvious to anyone who knows and loves the genre is that many favourite poems are missing from the pages that follow. So, conspicuously, there is no 'Ancient Mariner' to be found here, no 'Eve of St Agnes', no 'Goblin Market', no 'John Gilpin', no 'Pied Piper', no 'Horatius'. No extract, even, from *The Faerie Queene*, or *Paradise Lost*, or *Childe Harold*, or *The Borough* – those works of conscious heft and authority that, though none of them are quite epics by the standard definition, none-theless addressed the crises of their time through different forms of narrative, allegorical, tragic, high Romantic or realistic.

Insular English literature and the literatures that have grown from it are rich in the poetry of story-telling and continue to produce works on the grand scale, whether they are offered as epics, verse novels, or some other kind of thing. Passages might, for present purposes, have been excerpted from them, or from any number of the new translations or treatments of the classics that have been such a feature of recent English-language publishing, but I have left them out too. Partly, as with the omission of the Coleridge, Keats and Rossetti poems mentioned above, this has been decided by a consideration of space: I had no wish to end up creating a new monster genre, the epic anthology.

But there has been another reason for avoiding the more expansive, and sometimes – let's admit it – dismayingly verbose, schoolroom and golden-treasury war-horses. If the telling of a story has too often been seized by poets as an excuse for uninhibited elaboration and thumping explicitness, there is a counteracting force in the discipline of the verse line and the succinctness of both metaphor and metonymy, when they are successful, that can lead to marvels of economy, accuracy and suggestion. It is the second tendency which fascinates me and which I wanted to illuminate as I collected poems for this book.

Two of the key exhibits here are poems that most readers may never have thought of as concerned with story-telling in any significant way. Possibly, acceptance of this book as a whole will depend on whether these individual items are admitted to be part of the general picture. The poems I have in mind are Wyatt's 'They flee from me, that sometime did me seek' (included here on page 69) and Keats's 'On First Looking into Chapman's Homer' (page 138). The first is a love lyric, one that fits squarely into the sub-genre, complaint of the cruelly-used lover – if it isn't actually the poem by which all other such complaints are measured and judged. The second is a sonnet, on the firmly-established Italian model, but modernised by Keats to express, once and for all, the Romantic sense of joyous initiation into the world of the antique. Both poems are classics of their kind, standing out from the rest of their kind by virtue of certain distinctive and unforgettably registered details.

In Wyatt's case, the details contribute to an impact which is more than a matter of their accumulation. The plural pronoun 'They' in the first line, slyly qualified by a singular 'naked foot' in the next; the erotically choice 'loose gown' and 'arms long and small' of the second stanza; the complex emotional weight of the six little words quoted at the end of the same stanza; and the defiant 'It was no dream' in immediate reply – all these things have a sharpness and particularity which one stops short of calling 'novelistic' or 'cinematic', not just for fear of anachronism, but because it makes more sense to ask: 'Why shouldn't the love lyric contain such moments? Why should it be the domain, or dumping-ground, of stock attitudes and diction? Why must novels and movies have all the best tricks? Why must they have all the *stories?*' For a story is precisely what Wyatt's poem gives us: more than a series of emblematically striking details, through its balance of the particular and the undeclared, and through the uncanny pacing of three stanzas which might have been designed to stand for the 'beginning, middle and end' of the textbook narrative, it goes so much further, dramatically and emotionally, than its small scope might at first glimpse have promised. Knowing that Wyatt was a courtier possibly involved in amorous or political intrigue, and that the unnamed lover of the middle stanza may have been Anne Boleyn, conceivably lends an extra frisson to a reading of it, but does nothing to explain why the poem has lived for more than 400 years, while countless others by Wyatt's contemporaries, and by Wyatt himself, are now dusty and neglected.

Keats's sonnet is as candidly personal as the Wyatt poem is by subtle shades of rhetorical emphasis. It could even be described as anecdotal. It celebrates a revelatory moment in the life of the poet's imagination, the date of which we know, from documentary evidence, to be some time in October 1816; and its deliberately lofty diction, some of it – '... goodly ... bards ... fealty ... pure serene ...' – perilously close to fustian, is kept tied to reality, and explained as the product of spontaneous excitement, by the frequency with which the word 'I' occurs in the first nine lines. The first eight lines offer a fast-forward summary of Keats's reading of Homer, inevitably blurred in its details, while the final six – the sestet of the sonnet, where according to convention the development and conclusion of the poetic argument are conducted – present two parallel instances of an ostensibly static nature, which paradoxically give us the poem's true drama through their astounding precision, vividness and sense of imaginative embrace. What Keats, with the opportunistic flair of genius, has done is to identify in the Homeric metaphor, with its internal proliferations, the life and soul of all Homer's narrative. Then, by lifting the device from its classical habitat and seeing how it will thrive in the landscape of private experience, he shows that, in Romantic art, the personal may be elevated to the level of epic and his own small story be placed next to Homer's big one. As both a commentary on story-telling and an object-lesson in it, 'On First Looking into Chapman's Homer' is without equal. It is also central to the concerns of this anthology.

Narrative and lyric elements are not always so difficult to separate in the poems I have assembled here. Alongside those that prize the isolated but telling detail, the concealed connection, the unstated ending, the moment of metaphorical implication, or the image that conveys the sweep of an entire narrative journey, are those that go about their business quite openly and straightforwardly. Even there, however, economy of means has been a paramount consideration, and whatever aesthetic pleasure the poet has provided through his or her answer to the problem of balancing competing needs within tight limits – pace against authenticating detail and the sheer pleasure of embellishment; the pull of the narrative line against the constraints of the verse one – has clinched the matter. If any generalisation can be made about these 101 highly varied performances, it is that they all happen somewhere in, or close to, the region where narrative and lyric cross. As I went looking for them in that neck of the woods, I soon decided that no poem I brought home was to be longer than three pages, but that they must all satisfy me as having given complete and believable accounts of whatever it was, truth or fiction, that the writer had set out to tell us.

Because both truth and fiction are involved, it has to be admitted that a broad and perhaps incommunicably subjective definition of credibility is involved here. If so, let it be. I wanted this to be a capacious book in other respects, with room for both the comic and the tragic, the literal and the parabolic, the earthy and the visionary, the romantic and the sceptical, the thrilling and the enigmatic. Likewise with the readily accepted and the outlandish. Whether the reader believes, with the kind of belief required, the shaggy-dog story by Louis MacNeice with which I open my selection and from which the title of this volume is taken; or that Death did stop for Emily Dickinson, as she blithely announces in my second poem; or that the monks of Clonmacnoise were visited by a ship from the sky, as described by Seamus Heaney in his more guarded account, next – such questions depend for their answer on a complex of responses that will be different for every reader and beyond rational analysis anyway.

These introductory poems pose the problem of belief in extreme form. They remind us that one of the most remarkable features of story-telling itself, as a piece of human social behaviour, is that it involves teller and listener, writer and reader, in a highly precarious relationship. The least slip, whether of artistic miscalculation on one side, or of any number of failures to respond on the other, destroys everything. Yet, when the relationship holds true, the wildest invention, the assertion least amenable to objective verification, the tallest tale, can be believed. Why? Most systems of analysis deal well enough with the surrounding questions, but this central one of belief remains stubbornly difficult to get at. What is plain, though, is that the opportunity to believe, held out by any beguiling story-teller and seized by the trusting reader, is an unbeatable pleasure, all the more intense for the piquant awareness, not necessarily at a conscious level, of the many hazards to the enterprise that may be lying in wait.

Not to Speak of the Dog gathers the work of story-tellers who have taken the risk – and heightened it by choosing verse as their medium. They are not all concerned with the tallest tales, but even the most down-to-earth narratives require, in the space allowed by a short poem, skills of timing and nimble emphasis, acute instincts and a lot of luck. These poets cover a great range, chronologically, culturally and artistically. The oldest poem here (page 88) was written by Ovid in the first century A D, and translated with gusto by Christopher Marlowe in the sixteenth, so it will be understood that I have admitted items in translation when the translator has made a living English poem of the job. My shortest (page 22), similarly a work of translation, consists of three lines from the Japanese, cruelly curt in their ironic impact.* Elsewhere, poems in strict form and metre mingle with those that are freer, as do longer with shorter, and old with new; but I have tried

* My thanks to John Gross for showing me this.

[xiv]

to arrange them so that shared themes and contrasting treatments come to the fore. There is no intention – there was never any possibility – of offering this book as a complete statement on the subject, and a reading from start to finish is not necessarily recommended, but to approach groups of poems, if not the entire run, with a sense of how they might, between them, generate local currents and eddies of argument and accord should be, not just an academic exercise, but an enjoyable one. The first and most important thing, though, is to take each poem on its own, unique terms: an effort of exclusive concentration which, if I am right in placing the value I do on all 101 included here, should not be strenuous and will certainly be rewarded.

NOT TO SPEAK OF THE DOG

The Taxis

In the first taxi he was alone tra-la,
No extras on the clock. He tipped ninepence
But the cabby, while he thanked him, looked askance
As though to suggest someone had bummed a ride.

In the second taxi he was alone tra-la
But the clock showed sixpence extra; he tipped according
And the cabby from out his muffler said: 'Make sure
You have left nothing behind tra-la between you.'

In the third taxi he was alone tra-la
But the tip-up seats were down and there was an extra
Charge of one-and-sixpence and an odd
Scent that reminded him of a trip to Cannes.

As for the fourth taxi, he was alone
Tra-la when he hailed it but the cabby looked
Through him and said: 'I can't tra-la well take
So many people, not to speak of the dog.'

'Because I could not stop for Death'

Because I could not stop for Death—
He kindly stopped for me—
The Carriage held but just Ourselves—
And Immortality.

We slowly drove—He knew no haste
And I had put away
My labor and my leisure too,
For His Civility—

We passed the School, where Children strove
At Recess—in the Ring—
We passed the Fields of Gazing Grain—
We passed the Setting Sun—

Or rather—He passed Us—
The Dews drew quivering and chill—
For only Gossamer, my Gown—
My Tippet—only Tulle—

We paused before a House that seemed
A Swelling of the Ground—
The Roof was scarcely visible—
The Cornice—in the Ground—

Since then—'tis Centuries—and yet
Feels shorter than the Day
I first surmised the Horses Heads
Were toward Eternity—

SEAMUS HEANEY

'The annals say:
when the monks of Clonmacnoise'

The annals say: when the monks of Clonmacnoise
Were all at prayers inside the oratory
A ship appeared above them in the air.

The anchor dragged along behind so deep
It hooked itself into the altar rails
And then, as the big hull rocked to a standstill,

A crewman shinned and grappled down the rope
And struggled to release it. But in vain.
'This man can't bear our life here and will drown,'

The abbot said, 'unless we help him.' So
They did, the freed ship sailed, and the man climbed back
Out of the marvellous as he had known it.

from 'Squarings'

The Ferryman's Arms

About to sit down with my half-pint of Guinness
I was magnetized by a remote phosphorescence
and drawn, like a moth, to the darkened back room
where a pool-table hummed to itself in the corner.
With ten minutes to kill and the whole place deserted
I took myself on for the hell of it. Slotting
a coin in the tongue, I looked round for a cue –
while I stood with my back turned, the balls were deposited
with an abrupt intestinal rumble; a striplight
batted awake in its dusty green cowl.
When I set down the cue-ball inside the parched D
it clacked on the slate; the nap was so threadbare
I could screw back the globe, given somewhere to stand –
as physics itself becomes something negotiable
a rash of small miracles covers the shortfall:
I went on to make an immaculate clearance.
A low punch with a wee dab of side, and the black
did the vanishing trick while the white stopped
before gently rolling back as if nothing had happened,
shouldering its way through the unpotted colours.

The boat chugged up to the little stone jetty
without breaking the skin of the water, stretching,
as black as my stout, from somewhere unspeakable
to here, where the foaming lip mussitates endlessly,
trying, with a nutter's persistence, to read
and re-read the shoreline. I got aboard early,
remembering the ferry would leave on the hour

even for only my losing opponent;
but I left him there, stuck in his tent of light, sullenly
knocking the balls in, for practice, for next time.

Strange Meeting

It seemed that out of battle I escaped
Down some profound dull tunnel, long since scooped
Through granites which titanic wars had groined.
Yet also there encumbered sleepers groaned,
Too fast in thought or death to be bestirred.
Then, as I probed them, one sprang up, and stared
With piteous recognition in fixed eyes,
Lifting distressful hands as if to bless.
And by his smile, I knew that sullen hall,
By his dead smile I knew we stood in Hell.
With a thousand pains that vision's face was grained;
Yet no blood reached there from the upper ground,
And no guns thumped, or down the flues made moan.
'Strange friend,' I said, 'here is no cause to mourn.'
'None,' said the other, 'save the undone years,
The hopelessness. Whatever hope is yours,
Was my life also; I went hunting wild
After the wildest beauty in the world,
Which lies not calm in eyes, or braided hair,
But mocks the steady running of the hour,
And if it grieves, grieves richlier than here.
For by my glee might many men have laughed,
And of my weeping something had been left,
Which must die now. I mean the truth untold,
The pity of war, the pity war distilled.
Now men will go content with what we spoiled.
Or, discontent, boil bloody, and be spilled.
They will be swift with swiftness of the tigress,
None will break ranks, though nations trek from progress.

Courage was mine, and I had mystery,
Wisdom was mine, and I had mastery;
To miss the march of this retreating world
Into vain citadels that are not walled.
Then, when much blood had clogged their chariot-wheels
I would go up and wash them from sweet wells,
Even with truths that lie too deep for taint.
I would have poured my spirit without stint
But not through wounds; not on the cess of war.
Foreheads of men have bled where no wounds were.
I am the enemy you killed, my friend.
I knew you in this dark; for so you frowned
Yesterday through me as you jabbed and killed.
I parried; but my hands were loath and cold.
Let us sleep now . . .'

The Badger

The badger grunting on his woodland track
With shaggy hide and sharp nose scrowed with black
Roots in the bushes and the woods and makes
A great hugh burrow in the ferns and brakes
With nose on ground he runs a awkard pace
And anything will beat him in the race
The shepherds dog will run him to his den
Followed and hooted by the dogs and men
The woodman when the hunting comes about
Go round at night to stop the foxes out
And hurrying through the bushes ferns and brakes
Nor sees the many holes the badger makes
And often through the bushes to the chin
Breaks the old holes and tumbles headlong in.

When midnight comes a host of dogs and men
Go out and track the badger to his den
And put a sack within the hole and lye
Till the old grunting badger passes bye
He comes and hears they let the strongest loose
The old fox hears the noise and drops the goose
The poacher shoots and hurrys from the cry
And the old hare half wounded buzzes bye
They get a forked stick to bear him down
And clapt the dogs and bore him to the town
And bait him all the day with many dogs
And laugh and shout and fright the scampering hogs
He runs along and bites at all he meets
They shout and hollo down the noisey streets.

He turns about to face the loud uproar
And drives the rebels to their very doors
The frequent stone is hurled where ere they go
When badgers fight and every ones a foe
The dogs are clapt and urged to join the fray
The badger turns and drives them all away
Though scarcely half as big dimute and small
He fights with dogs for hours and beats them all
The heavy mastiff savage in the fray
Lies down and licks his feet and turns away
The bull dog knows his match and waxes cold
The badger grins and never leaves his hold
He drives the crowd and follows at their heels
And bites them though the drunkard swears and reels.

The frighted women takes the boys away
The blackguard laughs and hurrys on the fray
He tries to reach the woods a awkard race
But sticks and cudgels quickly stop the chace
He turns agen and drives the noisey crowd
And beats the many dogs in noises loud
He drives away and beats them every one
And then they loose them all and set them on
He falls as dead and kicked by boys and men
Then starts and grins and drives the crowd agen
Till kicked and torn and beaten out he lies
And leaves his hold and cackles groans and dies.

Some keep a baited badger tame as hog
And tame him till he follows like the dog
They urge him on like dogs and show fair play
He beats and scarcely wounded goes away
Lapt up as if asleep he scorns to fly
And siezes any dog that ventures nigh

[11]

Clapt like a dog he never bites the men
But worrys dogs and hurrys to his den
They let him out and turn a harrow down
And there he fights the host of all the town
He licks the patting hand and trys to play
And never trys to bite or run away
And runs away from noise in hollow trees
Burnt by the boys to get a swarm of bees.

Love on the Farm

What large, dark hands are those at the window
Grasping in the golden light
Which weaves its way through the evening wind
    At my heart's delight?

Ah, only the leaves! But in the west
I see a redness suddenly come
Into the evening's anxious breast—
    'Tis the wound of love goes home!

The woodbine creeps abroad
Calling low to her lover:
    The sun-lit flirt who all the day
    Has poised above her lips in play
    And stolen kisses, shallow and gay
    Of pollen, now has gone away—
    She woos the moth with her sweet, low word;
And when above her his moth-wings hover
Then her bright breast she will uncover
And yield her honey-drop to her lover.

Into the yellow, evening glow
Saunters a man from the farm below;
Leans, and looks in at the low-built shed
Where the swallow has hung her marriage bed.
    The bird lies warm against the wall.
    She glances quick her startled eyes
    Towards him, then she turns away
    Her small head, making warm display
    Of red upon the throat. Her terrors sway
    Her out of the nest's warm, busy ball,

Whose plaintive cry is heard as she flies
In one blue stoop from out the sties
Into the twilight's empty hall.

Oh, water-hen, beside the rushes
Hide your quaintly scarlet blushes,
Still your quick tail, lie still as dead,
Till the distance folds over his ominous tread!

The rabbit presses back her ears,
Turns back her liquid, anguished eyes
And crouches low; then with wild spring
Spurts from the terror of *his* oncoming;
To be choked back, the wire ring
Her frantic effort throttling:
    Piteous brown ball of quivering fears!
Ah, soon in his large, hard hands she dies,
And swings all loose from the swing of his walk!
Yet calm and kindly are his eyes
And ready to open in brown surprise
Should I not answer to his talk
Or should he my tears surmise.

I hear his hand on the latch, and rise from my chair
Watching the door open; he flashes bare
His strong teeth in a smile, and flashes his eyes
In a smile like triumph upon me; then careless-wise
He flings the rabbit soft on the table board
And comes towards me: ah! the uplifted sword
Of his hand against my bosom! and oh, the broad
Blade of his glance that asks me to applaud
His coming! With his hand he turns my face to him
And caresses me with his fingers that still smell grim
Of the rabbit's fur! God, I am caught in a snare!

I know not what fine wire is round my throat;
I only know I let him finger there
My pulse of life, and let him nose like a stoat
Who sniffs with joy before he drinks the blood.

And down his mouth comes to my mouth! and down
His bright dark eyes come over me, like a hood
Upon my mind! his lips meet mine, and a flood
Of sweet fire sweeps across me, so I drown
Against him, die, and find death good.

The Prodigal

The brown enormous odor he lived by
was too close, with its breathing and thick hair,
for him to judge. The floor was rotten; the sty
was plastered halfway up with glass-smooth dung.
Light-lashed, self-righteous, above moving snouts,
the pigs' eyes followed him, a cheerful stare –
even to the sow that always ate her young –
till, sickening, he leaned to scratch her head.
But sometimes mornings after drinking bouts
(he hid the pints behind a two-by-four),
the sunrise glazed the barnyard mud with red;
the burning puddles seemed to reassure.
And then he thought he almost might endure
his exile yet another year or more.

But evenings the first star came to warn.
The farmer whom he worked for came at dark
to shut the cows and horses in the barn
beneath their overhanging clouds of hay,
with pitchforks, faint forked lightnings, catching light,
safe and companionable as in the Ark.
The pigs stuck out their little feet and snored.
The lantern – like the sun, going away –
laid on the mud a pacing aureole.
Carrying a bucket along a slimy board,
he felt the bats' uncertain staggering flight,
his shuddering insights, beyond his control,
touching him. But it took him a long time
finally to make his mind up to go home.

EZRA POUND

The Gypsy

'Est-ce que vous avez vu des autres—des camarades—avec des singes ou des ours?'   A Stray Gipsy, AD 1912

That was the top of the walk, when he said:
'Have you seen any others, any of our lot,
With apes or bears?'
      —A brown upstanding fellow
Not like the half-castes,
      up on the wet road near Clermont.
The wind came, and the rain,
And mist clotted about the trees in the valley,
And I'd the long ways behind me,
      gray Arles and Biaucaire,
And he said, 'Have you seen any of our lot?'
I'd seen a lot of his lot . . .
      ever since Rhodez,
Coming down from the fair
      of St John,
With caravans, but never an ape or a bear.

The Player Queen's Wife

Our stage was Europe,
dragging from country to country
in a cart sold off by a rain-broken farmer
and trusting to the company's seven languages
(Garbo, a Gypsy and our Fool, had four of them).

A life spent trailing a cart
or, pregnant again, bouncing inside it
on a mattress of dusty curtains;
a life of haggling with innkeepers;
of naming the yearly children
after old Gods and dead actors;
of days stalled by a river
waiting for it to go down,
brown water thrashing like an animal's back.

And then, having come through mountains
or reached the steepled horizon across the plain
or that castle up on its crags
where the creeping Jesus in black
told us our own job – with actions –
once we'd arrived and unpacked,
made our bargain and beaten our drum,
I'd watch a stubbly queen
make me presents of myself:
daydreaming, she'd stop half-way
through pulling up a stocking
(as I've done, thinking of home)
or, laughing, splay her fringe (the best wig)
with a gesture I've had since a girl

or finally, at the bows and curtsies,
she'd grin and lift her skirts
to show again the stockings
I thought I'd lost two towns ago.

At Evening

Arriving early, I catch sight of you
Across the lawn. You're hovering:
A silver teaspoon in one hand
(The garden table almost set)
And in the other, a blue vase.
For the few seconds I stand watching you
It seems half-certain you'll choose wrong
– Well, not exactly wrong, but dottily,
Off-key. You know,
That dreaminess in you we used to smile about
(My pet, my little lavender, my sprite),
It's getting worse.
I'd talk to you about it if I could.

ANNA AKHMATOVA

'Three things enchanted him'

Three things enchanted him:
white peacocks, evensong,
and faded maps of America.
He couldn't stand bawling brats,
or raspberry jam with his tea,
or womanish hysteria.
. . . And he was married to me.

translated from the Russian
by Stanley Kunitz and Max Hayward

ANONYMOUS (18th century)

'In the whole village'

In the whole village
The husband alone
Does not know of it.

translated from the Japanese
by Geoffrey Bownas and Anthony Thwaite

ANONYMOUS

The Cherry-Tree Carol

Joseph was an old man,
    And an old man was he,
When he wedded Mary
    In the land of Galilee.

Joseph and Mary walked
    Through an orchard good,
Where was cherries and berries
    So red as any blood.

Joseph and Mary walked
    Through an orchard green,
Where was berries and cherries
    As thick as might be seen.

O then bespoke Mary
    So meek and so mild,
Pluck me one cherry, Joseph,
    For I am with child.

O then bespoke Joseph
    With words most unkind,
Let him pluck thee a cherry
    That brought thee with child.

O then bespoke the Babe
    Within his Mother's womb,
Bow down then the tallest tree
    For my Mother to have some.

Then bowed down the highest tree
    Unto his Mother's hand.
Then she cried, See, Joseph,
    I have cherries at command.

O then bespake Joseph,
    I have done Mary wrong,
But cheer up, my dearest,
    And be not cast down.

Then Mary plucked a cherry
    As red as the blood,
Then Mary went home
    With her heavy load.

Then Mary took her Babe
    And sat him on her knee,
Saying, My dear Son, tell me
    What this world will be.

O I shall be as dead, Mother,
    As the stones in the wall,
O the stones in the streets, Mother,
    Shall mourn for me all.

Upon Easter-day, Mother,
    My uprising shall be,
O the sun and the moon, Mother,
    Shall both rise with me.

T. S. ELIOT

Journey of the Magi

'A cold coming we had of it,
Just the worst time of the year
For a journey, and such a long journey:
The ways deep and the weather sharp,
The very dead of winter.'
And the camels galled, sore-footed, refractory,
Lying down in the melting snow.
There were times we regretted
The summer palaces on slopes, the terraces,
And the silken girls bringing sherbet.
Then the camel men cursing and grumbling
And running away, and wanting their liquor and women,
And the night-fires going out, and the lack of shelters,
And the cities hostile and the towns unfriendly
And the villages dirty and charging high prices:
A hard time we had of it.
At the end we preferred to travel all night,
Sleeping in snatches,
With the voices singing in our ears, saying
That this was all folly.

    Then at dawn we came down to a temperate valley,
Wet, below the snow line, smelling of vegetation,
With a running stream and a water-mill beating the
    darkness,
And three trees on the low sky.
And an old white horse galloped away in the meadow.
Then we came to a tavern with vine-leaves over the lintel,
Six hands at an open door dicing for pieces of silver,
And feet kicking the empty wine-skins.

But there was no information, and so we continued
And arrived at evening, not a moment too soon
Finding the place; it was (you may say) satisfactory.

　　All this was a long time ago, I remember,
And I would do it again, but set down
This set down
This: were we led all that way for
Birth or Death? There was a Birth, certainly,
We had evidence and no doubt. I had seen birth and death,
But had thought they were different; this Birth was
Hard and bitter agony for us, like Death, our death.
We returned to our places, these Kingdoms,
But no longer at ease here, in the old dispensation,
With an alien people clutching their gods.
I should be glad of another death.

In the Kalahari Desert

The sun rose like a tarnished
looking-glass to catch the sun

and flash His hot message
at the missionaries below—

Isabella and the Rev. Roger Price,
and the Helmores with a broken axle

left, two days behind, at Fever Ponds.
The wilderness was full of home:

a glinting beetle on its back
struggled like an orchestra

with Beethoven. The Hallé,
Isabella thought and hummed.

Makololo, their Zulu guide,
puzzled out the Bible, replacing

words he didn't know with Manchester.
Spikenard, alabaster, Leviticus,

were Manchester and Manchester.
His head reminded Mrs Price

of her old pomander stuck with cloves,
forgotten in some pungent tallboy.

The dogs drank under the wagon
with a far away clip-clopping sound,

and Roger spat into the fire,
leaned back and watched his phlegm

like a Welsh rarebit
bubbling on the brands . . .

When Baby died, they sewed her
in a scrap of carpet and prayed,

with milk still darkening
Isabella's grubby button-through.

Makololo was sick next day
and still the Helmores didn't come.

The outspanned oxen moved away
at night in search of water,

were caught and goaded on
to Matabele water-hole—

nothing but a dark stain on the sand.
Makololo drank vinegar and died.

Back they turned for Fever Ponds
and found the Helmores on the way . . .

Until they got within a hundred yards,
the vultures bobbed and trampolined

around the bodies, then swirled
a mile above their heads

like scalded tea leaves.
The Prices buried everything—

all the tattered clothes and flesh,
Mrs Helmore's bright chains of hair,

were wrapped in bits of calico
then given to the sliding sand.

'In the beginning was the Word' —
Roger read from Helmore's Bible

found open at St John.
Isabella moved her lips,

'The Word was Manchester'.
Shhh, shhh, the shovel said. Shhh . . .

In the Wilderness

He, of his gentleness,
Thirsting and hungering
Walked in the wilderness;
Soft words of grace he spoke
Unto lost desert-folk
That listened wondering.
He heard the bittern call
From ruined palace-wall,
Answered him brotherly;
He held communion
With the she-pelican
Of lonely piety.
Basilisk, cockatrice,
Flocked to his homilies,
With mail of dread device,
With monstrous barbèd stings,
With eager dragon-eyes;
Great bats on leathern wings
And old, blind, broken things
Mean in their miseries.
Then ever with him went,
Of all his wanderings
Comrade, with ragged coat,
Gaunt ribs – poor innocent –
Bleeding foot, burning throat,
The guileless young scapegoat:
For forty nights and days

Followed in Jesus' ways,
Sure guard behind him kept,
Tears like a lover wept.

GEORGE MACBETH

The God of Love

The musk-ox is accustomed to near-Arctic conditions. When danger
threatens, these beasts cluster together to form a defensive wall or
a 'porcupine' with the calves in the middle.
                                    Dr Wolfgang Engelhardt, *Survival of the Free*

I found them between far hills, by a frozen lake,
     On a patch of bare ground. They were grouped
In a solid ring, like an ark of horn. And around
     Them circled, slowly closing in,
Their tongues lolling, their ears flattened against the wind,

A whirlpool of wolves. As I breathed, one fragment of
          bone and
     Muscle detached itself from the mass and
Plunged. The pad of the pack slackened, as if
     A brooch had been loosened. But when the bull
Returned to the herd, the revolving collar was tighter.
          And only

The windward owl, uplifted on white wings
     In the glass of air, alert for her young,
Soared high enough to look into the cleared centre
     And grasp the cause. To the slow brain
Of each beast by the frozen lake what lay in the cradle of
          their crowned

Heads of horn was a sort of god-head. Its brows
     Nudged when the ark was formed. Its need
Was a delicate womb away from the iron collar
     Of death, a cave in the ring of horn
Their encircling flesh had backed with fur. That the collar
          of death

[32]

Was the bone of their own skulls: that a softer womb
    Would open between far hills in a plunge
Of bunched muscles: and that their immortal calf lay
    Dead on the snow with its horns dug into
The ice for grass: they neither saw nor felt. And yet if

That hill of fur could split and run – like a river
    Of ice in thaw, like a broken grave –
It would crack across the icy crust of withdrawn
    Sustenance and the rigid circle
Of death be shivered: the fed herd would entail its under-fur

On the swell of a soft hill and the future be sown
    On grass, I thought. But the herd fell
By the bank of the lake on the plain, and the pack closed,
    And the ice remained. And I saw that the god
In their ark of horn was a god of love, who made them die.

The Horses

Barely a twelvemonth after
The seven days war that put the world to sleep,
Late in the evening the strange horses came.
By then we had made our covenant with silence,
But in the first few days it was so still
We listened to our breathing and were afraid.
On the second day
The radios failed; we turned the knobs; no answer.
On the third day a warship passed us, heading north,
Dead bodies piled on the deck. On the sixth day
A plane plunged over us into the sea. Thereafter
Nothing. The radios dumb;
And still they stand in corners of our kitchens,
And stand, perhaps, turned on, in a million rooms
All over the world. But now if they should speak,
If on a sudden they should speak again,
If on the stroke of noon a voice should speak,
We would not listen, we would not let it bring
That old bad world that swallowed its children quick
At one great gulp. We would not have it again.
Sometimes we think of the nations lying asleep,
Curled blindly in impenetrable sorrow,
And then the thought confounds us with its strangeness.
The tractors lie about our fields; at evening
They look like dank sea-monsters couched and waiting.
We leave them where they are and let them rust:
'They'll moulder away and be like other loam'.
We make our oxen drag our rusty ploughs,
Long laid aside. We have gone back

Far past our fathers' land.

                           And then, that evening
Late in the summer the strange horses came.
We heard a distant tapping on the road,
A deepening drumming; it stopped, went on again
And at the corner changed to hollow thunder.
We saw the heads
Like a wild wave charging and were afraid.
We had sold our horses in our fathers' time
To buy new tractors. Now they were strange to us
As fabulous steeds set on an ancient shield
Or illustrations in a book of knights.
We did not dare go near them. Yet they waited,
Stubborn and shy, as if they had been sent
By an old command to find our whereabouts
And that long-lost archaic companionship.
In the first moment we had never a thought
That they were creatures to be owned and used.
Among them were some half-a-dozen colts
Dropped in some wilderness of the broken world,
Yet new as if they had come from their own Eden.
Since then they have pulled our ploughs and borne our loads
But that free servitude still can pierce our hearts.
Our life is changed; their coming our beginning.

Waiting for the Barbarians

What are we waiting for, assembled in the forum?

   The barbarians are due here today.

Why isn't anything going on in the senate?
Why are the senators sitting there without legislating?

   Because the barbarians are coming today.
   What's the point of senators making laws now?
   Once the barbarians are here, they'll do the legislating.

Why did our emperor get up so early,
and why is he sitting enthroned at the city's main gate,
in state, wearing the crown?

   Because the barbarians are coming today
   and the emperor's waiting to receive their leader.
   He's even got a scroll to give him,
   loaded with titles, with imposing names.

Why have our two consuls and praetors come out today
wearing their embroidered, their scarlet togas?
Why have they put on bracelets with so many amethysts,
rings sparkling with magnificent emeralds?
Why are they carrying elegant canes
beautifully worked in silver and gold?

   Because the barbarians are coming today
   and things like that dazzle the barbarians.

Why don't our distinguished orators turn up as usual
to make their speeches, say what they have to say?

Because the barbarians are coming today
and they're bored by rhetoric and public speaking.

Why this sudden bewilderment, this confusion?
(How serious people's faces have become.)
Why are the streets and squares emptying so rapidly,
everyone going home lost in thought?

Because night has fallen and the barbarians haven't come.
And some of our men just in from the border say
there are no barbarians any longer.

Now what's going to happen to us without barbarians?
Those people were a kind of solution.

translated from the Greek
by Edmund Keeley and Philip Sherrard

Love from a Foreign City

Dearest, the cockroaches are having babies.
One fell from the ceiling into my gin
with no ill effects. Mother has been.
I showed her the bite marks on the cot
and she gave me the name of her rat-catcher.
He was so impressed by the hole in her u-bend,
he took it home for his personal museum.
I cannot sleep. They are digging up children
on Hackney Marshes. The papers say
when that girl tried to scream for help,
the man cut her tongue out. Not far from here.
There have been more firebombs,
but only at dawn and out in the suburbs.
And a mortar attack. We heard it from the flat,
a thud like someone dropping a table.
They say the pond life coming out of the taps
is completely harmless. A law has been passed
on dangerous dogs: muzzles, tattoos, castration.
When the labrador over the road jumped up
to say hello to Billie, he wet himself.
The shops in North End Road are all closing.
You can't get your shoes mended anywhere.
The one-way system keeps changing direction,
I get lost a hundred yards from home.
There are parts of the new *A to* Z marked simply
'under development'. Even street names
have been demolished. There is typhoid in Finchley.
Mother has brought me a lavender tree.

A Chilly Night

I rose at the dead of night,
 And went to the lattice alone
To look for my Mother's ghost
 Where the ghostly moonlight shone.

My friends had failed one by one,
 Middle-aged, young, and old,
Till the ghosts were warmer to me
 Than my friends that had grown cold.

I looked and I saw the ghosts
 Dotting plain and mound:
They stood in the blank moonlight,
 But no shadow lay on the ground:
They spoke without a voice
 And they leaped without a sound.

I called: 'O my Mother dear,' —
 I sobbed: 'O my Mother kind,
Make a lonely bed for me
 And shelter it from the wind.

'Tell the others not to come
 To see me night or day:
But I need not tell my friends
 To be sure to keep away.'

My Mother raised her eyes,
 They were blank and could not see:
Yet they held me with their stare
 While they seemed to look at me.

She opened her mouth and spoke;
  I could not hear a word,
While my flesh crept on my bones
  And every hair was stirred.

She knew that I could not hear
  The message that she told
Whether I had long to wait
  Or soon should sleep in the mould:
I saw her toss her shadowless hair
  And wring her hands in the cold.

I strained to catch her words,
  And she strained to make me hear;
But never a sound of words
  Fell on my straining ear.

From midnight to the cockcrow
  I kept my watch in pain
While the subtle ghosts grew subtler
  In the sad night on the wane.

From midnight to the cockcrow
  I watched till all were gone,
Some to sleep in the shifting sea
  And some under turf and stone:
Living had failed and dead had failed,
  And I was indeed alone.

Vision by Sweetwater

Go and ask Robin to bring the girls over
To Sweetwater, said my Aunt; and that was why
It was like a dream of ladies sweeping by
The willows, clouds, deep meadowgrass, and river.

Robin's sisters and my Aunt's lily daughter
Laughed and talked, and tinkled light as wrens
If there were a little colony all hens
To go walking by the steep turn of Sweetwater.

Let them alone, dear Aunt, just for one minute
Till I go fishing in the dark of my mind:
Where have I seen before, against the wind,
These bright virgins, robed and bare of bonnet,

Flowing with music of their strange quick tongue
And adventuring with delicate paces by the stream,—
Myself a child, old suddenly at the scream
From one of the white throats which it hid among?

'There was a child went forth'

There was a child went forth every day,
And the first object he look'd upon, that object he became,
And that object became part of him for the day or a certain
    part of the day,
Or for many years or stretching cycles of years.

The early lilacs became part of this child,
And grass and white and red morning-glories, and white
    and red clover, and the song of the phoebe-bird,
And the Third-month lambs and the sow's pink-faint litter,
    and the mare's foal and the cow's calf,
And the noisy brood of the barnyard or by the mire of the
    pond-side,
And the fish suspending themselves so curiously below
    there, and the beautiful curious liquid,
And the water-plants with their graceful flat heads, all
    became part of him.

The field-sprouts of Fourth-month and Fifth-month
    became part of him,
Winter-grain sprouts and those of the light-yellow corn,
    and the esculent roots of the garden,
And the apple-trees cover'd with blossoms and the fruit
    afterward, and wood-berries, and the commonest weeds
    by the road,
And the old drunkard staggering home from the outhouse
    of the tavern whence he had lately risen,
And the schoolmistress that pass'd on her way to the
    school,
And the friendly boys that pass'd and the quarrelsome boys,

And the tidy and fresh-cheek'd girls, and the barefoot
	Negro boy and girl,
And all the changes of city and country wherever he went.

His own parents, he that had father'd him and she that had
	conceiv'd him in her womb and birth'd him,
They gave this child more of themselves than that,
They gave him afterward every day, they became part of him.
The mother at home quietly placing the dishes on the
	supper-table,
The mother with mild words, clean her cap and gown, a
	wholesome odor falling off her person and clothes as she
	walks by,
The father, strong, self-sufficient, manly, mean, anger'd,
	unjust,
The blow, the quick loud word, the tight bargain, the crafty
	lure,
The family usages, the language, the company, the
	furniture, the yearning and swelling heart,
Affection that will not be gainsay'd, the sense of what is
	real, the thought if after all it should prove unreal,
The doubts of day-time and the doubts of night-time, the
	curious whether and how,
Whether that which appears so is so, or is it all flashes and
	specks?
Men and women crowding fast in the streets, if they are not
	flashes and specks what are they?
The streets themselves and the façades of houses, and
	goods in the windows,
Vehicles, teams, the heavy-plank'd wharves, the huge
	crossing at the ferries,
The village on the highland seen from afar at sunset, the
	river between,

Shadows, aureola and mist, the light falling on roofs and
  gables of white or brown two miles off,
The schooner near by sleepily dropping down the tide, the
  little boat slack-tow'd astern,
The hurrying tumbling waves, quick-broken crests,
  slapping,
The strata of color'd clouds, the long bar of maroon-tint
  away solitary by itself, the spread of purity it lies
  motionless in,
The horizon's edge, the flying sea-crow, the fragrance of
  salt marsh and shore mud,
These became part of that child who went forth every day,
  and who now goes, and will always go forth every day.

Epitaph on Salomon Pavy, a Child of Queen Elizabeth's Chapel

Weep with me all you that read
   This little story,
And know, for whom a tear you shed,
   Death's self is sorry.
'Twas a child that so did thrive
   In grace and feature,
As heaven and nature seemed to strive
   Which owned the creature.
Years he numbered scarce thirteen
   When fates turned cruel,
Yet three filled zodiacs had he been
   The stage's jewel,
And did act (what now we moan)
   Old men so duly
As, sooth, the Parcae thought him one,
   He played so truly.
So, by error, to his fate
   They all consented,
But viewing him since (alas, too late)
   They have repented;
And have sought, to give new birth,
   In baths to steep him;
But being so much too good for earth,
   Heaven vows to keep him.

Lucy Gray
(or, Solitude)

Oft I had heard of Lucy Gray:
And, when I crossed the wild,
I chanced to see at break of day
The solitary child.

No mate, no comrade Lucy knew;
She dwelt on a wide moor,
—The sweetest thing that ever grew
Beside a human door!

You yet may spy the fawn at play,
The hare upon the green;
But the sweet face of Lucy Gray
Will never more be seen.

'To-night will be a stormy night—
You to the town must go;
And take a lantern, Child, to light
Your mother through the snow.'

'That, Father! will I gladly do:
'Tis scarcely afternoon—
The minster-clock has just struck two,
And yonder is the moon!'

At this the Father raised his hook,
And snapped a faggot-band;
He plied his work;—and Lucy took
The lantern in her hand.

No blither is the mountain roe:
With many a wanton stroke
Her feet disperse the powdery snow,
That rises up like smoke.

The storm came on before its time:
She wandered up and down;
And many a hill did Lucy climb:
But never reached the town.

The wretched parents all that night
Went shouting far and wide;
But there was neither sound nor sight
To serve them for a guide.

At day-break on a hill they stood
That overlooked the moor;
And thence they saw the bridge of wood,
A furlong from their door.

They wept—and, turning homeward, cried,
'In heaven we all shall meet;'
—When in the snow the mother spied
The print of Lucy's feet.

Then downwards from the steep hill's edge
They tracked the footmarks small;
And through the broken hawthorn hedge,
And by the long stone-wall;

And then an open field they crossed:
The marks were still the same;
They tracked them on, nor ever lost;
And to the bridge they came.

They followed from the snowy bank
Those footmarks, one by one,
Into the middle of the plank;
And further there were none!

—Yet some maintain that to this day
She is a living child;
That you may see sweet Lucy Gray
Upon the lonesome wild.

O'er rough and smooth she trips along,
And never looks behind;
And sings a solitary song
That whistles in the wind.

Stafford Afternoons

Only there, the afternoons could suddenly pause
and when I looked up from lacing my shoe
a long road held no one, the gardens were empty,
an ice-cream van chimed and dwindled away.

On the motorway bridge, I waved at windscreens,
oddly hurt by the blurred waves back, the speed.
So I let a horse in the noisy field sponge at my palm
and invented, in colour, a vivid lie for us both.

In a cul-de-sac, a strange boy threw a stone.
I crawled through a hedge into long grass
at the edge of a small wood, lonely and thrilled.
The green silence gulped once and swallowed me whole.

I knew it was dangerous. The way the trees
drew sly faces from light and shade, the wood
let out its sticky breath on the back of my neck,
and flowering nettles gathered spit in their throats.

Too late. *Touch*, said the long-haired man
who stood, legs apart, by a silver birch
with a living, purple root in his hand. The sight
made sound rush back; birds, a distant lawnmower,

his hoarse, frightful endearments as I backed away
then ran all the way home; into a game
where children scattered and shrieked
and time fell from the sky like a red ball.

I Remember, I Remember

Coming up England by a different line
For once, early in the cold new year,
We stopped, and, watching men with number-plates
Sprint down the platform to familiar gates,
'Why, Coventry!' I exclaimed. 'I was born here.'

I leant far out, and squinnied for a sign
That this was still the town that had been 'mine'
So long, but found I wasn't even clear
Which side was which. From where those cycle-crates
Were standing, had we annually departed

For all those family hols? . . . A whistle went:
Things moved. I sat back, staring at my boots.
'Was that,' my friend smiled, 'where you "have you roots"?'
No, only where my childhood was unspent,
I wanted to retort, just where I started:

By now I've got the whole place clearly charted.
Our garden, first: where I did not invent
Blinding theologies of flowers and fruits,
And wasn't spoken to by an old hat.
And here we have that splendid family

I never ran to when I got depressed,
The boys all biceps and the girls all chest,
Their comic Ford, their farm where I could be
'Really myself'. I'll show you, come to that,
The bracken where I never trembling sat,

Determined to go through with it; where she
Lay back, and 'all became a burning mist'.
And, in those offices, my doggerel
Was not set up in blunt ten-point, nor read
By a distinguished cousin of the mayor,

Who didn't call and tell my father *There*
Before us, had we the gift to see ahead –
'You look as if you wished the place in Hell,'
My friend said, 'judging from your face.' 'Oh well,
I suppose it's not the place's fault,' I said.

'Nothing, like something, happens anywhere.'

Nutting

It seems a day,
(I speak of one from many singled out)
One of those heavenly days which cannot die,
When forth I sallied from our cottage-door,
And with a wallet o'er my shoulder slung,
A nutting crook in hand, I turn'd my steps
Towards the distant woods, a Figure quaint,
Trick'd out in proud disguise of Beggar's weeds
Put on for the occasion, by advice
And exhortation of my frugal Dame.
Motley accoutrement! of power to smile
At thorns, and brakes, and brambles, and, in truth,
More ragged than need was. Among the woods,
And o'er the pathless rocks, I forc'd my way
Until, at length, I came to one dear nook
Unvisited, where not a broken bough
Droop'd with its wither'd leaves, ungracious sign
Of devastation, but the hazels rose
Tall and erect, with milk-white clusters hung,
A virgin scene!—A little while I stood,
Breathing with such suppression of the heart
As joy delights in; and with wise restraint
Voluptuous, fearless of a rival, eyed
The banquet, or beneath the trees I sate
Among the flowers, and with the flowers I play'd;
A temper known to those, who, after long
And weary expectation, have been bless'd
With sudden happiness beyond all hope.—
—Perhaps it was a bower beneath whose leaves

The violets of five seasons re-appear
And fade, unseen by any human eye,
Where fairy water-breaks do murmur on
For ever, and I saw the sparkling foam,
And with my cheek on one of those green stones
That, fleec'd with moss, beneath the shady trees,
Lay round me scatter'd like a flock of sheep,
I heard the murmur and the murmuring sound,
In that sweet mood when pleasure loves to pay
Tribute to ease, and, of its joy secure
The heart luxuriates with indifferent things,
Wasting its kindliness on stocks and stones,
And on the vacant air. Then up I rose,
And dragg'd to earth both branch and bough, with crash
And merciless ravage; and the shady nook
Of hazels, and the green and mossy bower
Deform'd and sullied, patiently gave up
Their quiet being: and unless I now
Confound my present feelings with the past,
Even then, when from the bower I turn'd away,
Exulting, rich beyond the wealth of kings
I felt a sense of pain when I beheld
The silent trees and the intruding sky.—

Then, dearest Maiden! move along these shades
In gentleness of heart; with gentle hand
Touch,—for there is a Spirit in the woods.

GEOFFREY LEHMANN

The Old Rifle

In the long school holidays in summer
I'd be out in the orchard
with an old rifle Mr Long fixed up,
shooting at rosellas
that were raiding fruit.
As each bird fell I'd watch
where the blue and red flickered down,
then I'd drop the rifle and run.
That way I stocked my aviary
with broken-winged rosellas.
And somewhere in my childhood
I dropped and forgot that rifle.

A year of grass grew over it.
Men were working in the orchard one day,
and my brother, the dentist, four years old,
was playing in the grass and found the rifle,
rusted all over – a wreck –
as though it had lain there for years.
My brother knew how to hold a gun
and pointing it at Jim Long, said,
'I'll shoot you Mr Long.'
He said, 'Oh don't shoot me, Barry –
shoot Bill over there.'
Barry pointed the gun at Bill.
'I'll shoot you Uncle Bill.'
'Don't shoot me, Barry,' Bill said,
'Shoot Ted here.' And Ted said,
'Why not shoot Jip?'

Jip was a good sort of dog,
my black and white fox terrier cross,
who was racing around the orchard,
looking for rabbits.
Barry dropped to one knee and squinting took aim.
Jip dropped dead on the spot.
They buried him, telling no one,
but in their haste
made the hole too shallow,
and a few days later the story came out
when the fowls scratched him up.

'You know, Barry's quite a fair shot,'
Mr Long said,
out in the bush with Barry and me.
'My word I am,' said Barry.
'I can hit anything.'
'Can you, Barry, well – see what you can do.'
Barry took the rifle,
went down on one knee
and aimed at Mr Long's billy hanging
from a distant branch.
He fired,
and a stream of brown tea came spurting out.

'Out, Out—'

The buzz-saw snarled and rattled in the yard
And made dust and dropped stove-length sticks of wood,
Sweet-scented stuff when the breeze drew across it.
And from there those that lifted eyes could count
Five mountain ranges one behind the other
Under the sunset far into Vermont.
And the saw snarled and rattled, snarled and rattled,
As it ran light, or had to bear a load.
And nothing happened: day was all but done.
Call it a day, I wish they might have said
To please the boy by giving him the half hour
That a boy counts so much when saved from work.
His sister stood beside them in her apron
To tell them 'Supper.' At the word, the saw,
As if to prove saws knew what supper meant,
Leaped out at the boy's hand, or seemed to leap—
He must have given the hand. However it was,
Neither refused the meeting. But the hand!
The boy's first outcry was a rueful laugh,
As he swung toward them holding up the hand
Half in appeal, but half as if to keep
The life from spilling. Then the boy saw all—
Since he was old enough to know, big boy
Doing a man's work, though a child at heart—
He saw all spoiled. 'Don't let him cut my hand off—
The doctor, when he comes. Don't let him, sister!'
So. But the hand was gone already.
The doctor put him in the dark of ether.
He lay and puffed his lips out with his breath.

[56]

And then—the watcher at his pulse took fright.
No one believed. They listened at his heart.
Little—less—nothing!—and that ended it.
No more to build on there. And they, since they
Were not the one dead, turned to their affairs.

Timothy Winters

Timothy Winters comes to school
With eyes as wide as a football pool,
Ears like bombs and teeth like splinters:
A blitz of a boy is Timothy Winters.

His belly is white, his neck is dark,
And his hair is an exclamation mark.
His clothes are enough to scare a crow
And through his britches the blue winds blow.

When teacher talks he won't hear a word
And he shoots down dead the arithmetic-bird,
He licks the patterns off his plate
And he's not even heard of the Welfare State.

Timothy Winters has bloody feet
And he lives in a house on Suez Street,
He sleeps in a sack on the kitchen floor
And they say there aren't boys like him any more.

Old Man Winters likes his beer
And his missus ran off with a bombardier,
Grandma sits in the grate with a gin
And Timothy's dosed with an aspirin.

The Welfare Worker lies awake,
But the law's as tricky as a ten-foot snake,
So Timothy Winters drinks his cup
And slowly goes on growing up.

At Morning Prayers the Master helves
For children less fortunate than ourselves,

And the loudest response in the room is when
Timothy Winters roars 'Amen!'

So come one angel, come on ten:
Timothy Winters says 'Amen
Amen amen amen amen.'
Timothy Winters, Lord.
                              Amen.

Not the Furniture Game

His hair was a crow fished out of a blocked chimney
and his eyes were boiled eggs with the tops hammered in
and his blink was a cat flap
and his teeth were bluestones or Easter Island statues
and his bite was a perfect horseshoe.
His nostrils were both barrels of a shotgun, loaded.
And his mouth was an oil exploration project gone
    bankrupt
and his last smile was a caesarean section
and his tongue was an iguanodon
and his whistle was a laser beam
and his laugh was a bad case of kennel cough.
He coughed, and it was malt whisky.
And his headaches were Arson in Her Majesty's Dockyards
and his arguments were outboard motors strangled with
    fishing-line
and his neck was a bandstand
and his Adam's apple was a ball cock
and his arms were milk running off from a broken bottle.
His elbows were boomerangs or pinking shears.
And his wrists were ankles
and his handshakes were puff adders in the bran tub
and his fingers were astronauts found dead in their
    spacesuits
and the palms of his hands were action paintings
and both thumbs were blue touchpaper.
And his shadow was an opencast mine.
And his dog was a sentry-box with no one in it

and his heart was a first world war grenade discovered by
    children
and his nipples were timers for incendiary devices
and his shoulder-blades were two butchers at the meat-
    cleaving competition
and his belly-button was the Falkland Islands
and his private parts were the Bermuda triangle
and his backside was a priest hole
and his stretchmarks were the tide going out.
The whole system of his blood was Dutch elm disease.
And his legs were depth charges
and his knees were fossils waiting to be tapped open
and his ligaments were rifles wrapped in oilcloth under the
    floorboards
and his calves were the undercarriages of Shackletons.
The balls of his feet were where meteorites had landed
and his toes were a nest of mice under the lawn-mower.
And his footprints were Vietnam
and his promises were hot-air balloons floating off over
    the trees
and his one-liners were footballs through other peoples'
    windows
and his grin was the Great Wall of China as seen from the
    moon
and the last time they talked, it was apartheid.

She was a chair, tipped over backwards
with his donkey jacket on her shoulders.

They told him,
and his face was a hole
where the ice had not been thick enough to hold her.

The Other

She had too much so with a smile you took some.
Of everything she had you had
Absolutely nothing, so you took some.
At first, just a little.

Still she had so much she made you feel
Your vacuum, which nature abhorred,
So you took your fill, for nature's sake.
Because her great luck made you feel unlucky
You had redressed the balance, which meant
Now you had some too, for yourself.
As seemed only fair. Still her ambition
Claimed the natural right to screw you up
Like a crossed-out page, tossed into a basket.
Somebody, on behalf of the gods,
Had to correct that hubris.
A little touch of hatred steadied the nerves.

Everything she had won, the happiness of it,
You collected
As your compensation
For having lost. Which left her absolutely
Nothing. Even her life was
Trapped in the heap you took. She had nothing.
Too late you saw what had happened.
It made no difference that she was dead.
Now that you had all she had ever had
You had much too much.
                         Only you

Saw her smile, as she took some.
At first, just a little.

'Cupid and my Campaspe played'

Cupid and my Campaspe played
At cards for kisses, Cupid paid;
He stakes his quiver, bow, and arrows,
His mother's doves, and team of sparrows;
Loses them too; then, down he throws
The coral of his lip, the rose
Growing on 's cheek (but none knows how);
With these, the crystal of his brow,
And then the dimple of his chin:
All these did my Campaspe win.
At last, he set her both his eyes;
She won, and Cupid blind did rise.
    O Love, has she done this to thee?
    What shall (alas) become of me?

Long John Brown and Little Mary Bell

Little Mary Bell had a Fairy in a Nut,
Long John Brown had the Devil in his Gut;
Long John Brown lov'd Little Mary Bell,
And the Fairy drew the Devil into the Nut-shell.

Her Fairy Skip'd out and her Fairy Skip'd in;
He laugh'd at the Devil saying 'Love is a Sin.'
The Devil he raged and the Devil he was wroth,
And the Devil enter'd into the Young Man's broth.

He was soon in the Gut of the loving Young Swain,
For John eat and drank to drive away Love's pain;
But all he could do he grew thinner and thinner,
Tho' he eat and drank as much as ten Men for his dinner.

Some said he had a Wolf in his stomach day and night,
Some said he had the Devil and they guess'd right;
The Fairy skip'd about in his Glory, Joy and Pride,
And he laugh'd at the Devil till poor John Brown died.

Then the Fairy skip'd out of the old Nut-shell,
And woe and alack for Pretty Mary Bell!
For the Devil crept in when the Fairy skip'd out,
And there goes Miss Bell with her fusty old Nut.

The Ecstasy

Where, like a pillow on a bed,
   A pregnant bank swell'd up, to rest
The violet's reclining head,
   Sat we two, one another's best.
Our hands were firmly cemented
   With a fast balm, which thence did spring,
Our eye-beams twisted, and did thread
   Our eyes, upon one double string;
So t' intergraft our hands, as yet
   Was all the means to make us one,
And pictures in our eyes to get
   Was all our propagation.
As 'twixt two equal Armies, Fate
   Suspends uncertain victory,
Our souls, (which to advance their state,
   Were gone out,) hung 'twixt her, and me.
And whilst our souls negotiate there,
   We like sepulchral statues lay;
All day, the same our postures were,
   And we said nothing, all the day.
If any, so by love refin'd,
   That he soul's language understood,
And by good love were grown all mind,
   Within convenient distance stood,
He (though he knew not which soul spake,
   Because both meant, both spake the same)
Might thence a new concoction take,
   And part far purer than he came.

This Ecstasy doth unperplex
	(We said) and tell us what we love,
We see, by this, it was not sex,
	We see, we saw not what did move:
But as all several souls contain
	Mixture of things, they know not what,
Love these mix'd souls doth mix again,
	And makes both one, each this and that.
A single violet transplant,
	The strength, the colour, and the size,
(All which before was poor, and scant,)
	Redoubles still, and multiplies.
When love, with one another so
	Interinanimates two souls,
That abler soul, which thence doth flow,
	Defects of loneliness controls.
We then, who are this new soul, know,
	Of what we are compos'd, and made,
For, th' Atomies of which we grow,
	Are souls, whom no change can invade.
But O alas, so long, so far
	Our bodies why do we forbear?
They are ours, though they are not we, We are
	The intelligences, they the spheres.
We owe them thanks, because they thus,
	Did us, to us, at first convey,
Yielded their forces, sense, to us,
	Nor are dross to us, but allay.
On man heaven's influence works not so,
	But that it first imprints the air,
So soul into the soul may flow,
	Though it to body first repair.

As our blood labours to beget
    Spirits, as like souls as it can,
Because such fingers need to knit
    That subtle knot, which makes us man:
So must pure lovers' souls descend
    T' affections, and to faculties,
Which sense may reach and apprehend,
    Else a great Prince in prison lies.
To our bodies turn we then, that so
    Weak men on love reveal'd may look;
Love's mysteries in souls do grow,
    But yet the body is his book,
And if some lover, such as we,
    Have heard this dialogue of one,
Let him still mark us, he shall see
    Small change, when we're to bodies gone.

'They flee from me, that sometime did me seek'

They flee from me, that sometime did me seek
With naked foot stalking in my chamber.
I have seen them gentle, tame, and meek
That now are wild, and do not remember
That sometime they put themself in danger
To take bread at my hand; and now they range,
Busily seeking with a continual change.

Thanked be fortune it hath been otherwise
Twenty times better, but once in special,
In thin array after a pleasant guise
When her loose gown from her shoulders did fall,
And she me caught in her arms long and small,
Therewithal sweetly did me kiss,
And softly said, 'Dear heart, how like you this?'

It was no dream; I lay broad waking.
But all is turned thorough my gentleness
Into a strange fashion of forsaking,
And I have leave to go of her goodness,
And she also to use newfangleness.
But since that I so kindly am served,
I would fain know what she hath deserved.

Water

It was a Maine lobster town—
each morning boatloads of hands
pushed off for granite
quarries on the islands,

and left dozens of bleak
white frame houses stuck
like oyster shells
on a hill of rock,

and below us, the sea lapped
the raw little match-stick
mazes of a weir,
where the fish for bait were trapped.

Remember? We sat on a slab of rock.
From this distance in time,
it seems the color
of iris, rotting and turning purpler,

but it was only
the usual gray rock
turning the usual green
when drenched by the sea.

The sea drenched the rock
at our feet all day,
and kept tearing away
flake after flake.

One night you dreamed
you were a mermaid clinging to a wharf-pile,
and trying to pull
off the barnacles with your hands.

We wished our two souls
might return like gulls
to the rock. In the end,
the water was too cold for us.

White Heliotrope

The feverish room and that white bed,
   The tumbled skirts upon a chair,
   The novel flung half-open, where
Hat, hair-pins, puffs, and paints, are spread;

The mirror that has sucked your face
   Into its secret deep of deeps,
   And there mysteriously keeps
Forgotten memories of grace;

And you, half dressed and half awake,
   Your slant eyes strangely watching me,
   And I, who watch you drowsily,
With eyes that, having slept not, ache;

This (need one dread? nay, dare one hope?)
   Will rise, a ghost of memory, if
   Ever again my handkerchief
Is scented with White Heliotrope.

Milk

This notebook in which he used to sketch
has, on its expensive-looking black cover,

a sprinkle of whitish stains: of the sort
sure to detain the unborn biographer.

Could they be the miniaturist's impression
of the northern sky, his Starry Night?

Or might lab-tests point to something else?
That they are, in fact, human milk-stains,

the effect of lactic acid on cheap skin,
and date from five years earlier –

a time when his wife's hyperactive glands
used to lob milk right across the room

to the wing-chair in which he dozed,
the sketchbook (it seems) closed in his hands.

Though he felt its light lash on his skin
many a night, he never took to that milk

and wished only for a wider room.
A failure of imagination, you might claim,

though it could be he needed more
of human kindness from that source then.

You could even say that the milk stopped,
but the acid didn't. That he replied in kind.

And thus it began: the pointless unstoppable game
across a room, in which a child grew

less small, and became the mesmerized umpire
looking now one way, now the other.

WILLIAM BLAKE

A Poison Tree

I was angry with my friend:
I told my wrath, my wrath did end.
I was angry with my foe:
I told it not, my wrath did grow.

And I water'd it in fears,
Night and morning with my tears;
And I sunned it with smiles,
And with soft deceitful wiles.

And it grew both day and night,
Till it bore an apple bright;
And my foe beheld it shine,
And he knew that it was mine,

And into my garden stole
When the night had veil'd the pole:
In the morning glad I see
My foe outstretch'd beneath the tree.

A. E. HOUSMAN

'Is my team ploughing'

'Is my team ploughing,
  That I was used to drive
And hear the harness jingle
  When I was man alive?'

Ay, the horses trample,
  The harness jingles now;
No change though you lie under
  The land you used to plough.

'Is football playing
  Along the river shore,
With lads to chase the leather,
  Now I stand up no more?'

Ay, the ball is flying,
  The lads play heart and soul;
The goal stands up, the keeper
  Stands up to keep the goal.

'Is my girl happy,
  That I thought hard to leave,
And has she tired of weeping
  As she lies down at eve?'

Ay, she lies down lightly,
  She lies not down to weep:
Your girl is well contented.
  Be still, my lad, and sleep.

'Is my friend hearty,
　　Now I am thin and pine,
And has he found to sleep in
　　A better bed than mine?'

Yes, lad, I lie easy,
　　I lie as lads would choose;
I cheer a dead man's sweetheart,
　　Never ask me whose.

ANONYMOUS

The Unquiet Grave

'The wind doth blow today, my love,
   And a few small drops of rain;
I never had but one true-love,
   In cold grave she was lain.

'I'll do as much for my true-love
   As any young man may;
I'll sit and mourn all at her grave
   For a twelvemonth and a day.'

The twelvemonth and a day being up,
   The dead began to speak:
'Oh who sits weeping on my grave,
   And will not let me sleep?'

''Tis I, my love, sits on your grave,
   And will not let you sleep;
For I crave one kiss of your clay-cold lips,
   And that is all I seek.'

'You crave one kiss of my clay-cold lips;
   But my breath smells earthy strong;
If you have one kiss of my clay-cold lips,
   Your time will not be long.

''Tis down in yonder garden green,
   Love, where we used to walk,
The finest flower that ere was seen
   Is withered to a stalk.

'The stalk is withered dry, my love,
  So will our hearts decay;
So make yourself content, my love,
  Till God calls you away.'

'Methought I saw my late espousèd saint'

Methought I saw my late espousèd saint
   Brought to me like Alcestis from the grave,
   Whom Jove's great son to her glad husband gave,
   Rescued from death by force though pale and faint.
Mine as whom washed from spot of childbed taint,
   Purification in the old Law did save,
   And such, as yet once more I trust to have
   Full sight of her in Heaven without restraint,
Came vested all in white, pure as her mind:
   Her face was veiled, yet to my fancied sight,
   Love, sweetness, goodness, in her person shined
So clear, as in no face with more delight.
   But O as to embrace me she inclined
   I waked, she fled, and day brought back my night.

The Reassurance

About ten days or so
After we saw you dead
You came back in a dream.
I'm all right now you said.

And it *was* you, although
You were fleshed out again:
You hugged us all round then,
And gave your welcoming beam.

How like you to be kind,
Seeking to reassure.
And, yes, how like my mind
To make itself secure.

The River-Merchant's Wife: A Letter

While my hair was still cut straight across my forehead
I played about the front gate, pulling flowers.
You came by on bamboo stilts, playing horse,
You walked about my seat, playing with blue plums.
And we went on living in the village of Chokan:
Two small people, without dislike or suspicion.

At fourteen I married My Lord you.
I never laughed, being bashful.
Lowering my head, I looked at the wall.
Called to, a thousand times, I never looked back.

At fifteen I stopped scowling,
I desired my dust to be mingled with yours
Forever and forever and forever.
Why should I climb the look out?

At sixteen you departed,
You went into far Ku-to-yen, by the river of swirling
  eddies,
And you have been gone five months.
The monkeys make sorrowful noise overhead.
You dragged your feet when you went out.
By the gate now, the moss is grown, the different mosses,
Too deep to clear them away!
The leaves fall early this autumn, in wind.
The paired butterflies are already yellow with August
Over the grass in the West garden;
They hurt me. I grow older.
If you are coming down through the narrows of the river
  Kiang,

Please let me know beforehand,
And I will come out to meet you
                As far as Cho-fu-Sa.

translated from the Chinese of Li Po

Meeting at Night

I

The grey sea and the long black land;
And the yellow half-moon large and low;
And the startled little waves that leap
In fiery ringlets from their sleep,
As I gain the cove with pushing prow,
And quench its speed i' the slushy sand.

II

Then a mile of warm sea-scented beach;
Three fields to cross till a farm appears;
A tap at the pane, the quick sharp scratch
And blue spurt of a lighted match,
And a voice less loud, thro' its joys and fears,
Than the two hearts beating each to each!

Wulf and Eadwacer

The men of my tribe would treat him as game:
if he comes to the camp they will kill him outright.

>   Our fate is forked.

Wulf is on one island, I on another.
Mine is a fastness: the fens girdle it
and it is defended by the fiercest men.
If he comes to the camp they will kill him for sure.

>   Our fate is forked.

It was rainy weather, and I wept by the hearth,
thinking of my Wulf's far wanderings;
one of the captains caught me in his arms.
It gladdened me then; but it grieved me too.

Wulf, my Wulf, it was wanting you
that made me sick, your seldom coming,
the hollowness at heart; not the hunger I spoke of.

Do you hear, Eadwacer? Our whelp
>   Wulf shall take to the wood.
What was never bound is broken easily,
>   our song together.

translated from the Old English
by Michael Alexander

Young Lochinvar

O, young Lochinvar is come out of the West!
Through all the wide Border his steed is the best;
And save his good broadsword he weapon had none;
He rode all unarm'd and he rode all alone.
So faithful in love, and so dauntless in war,
There never was knight like the young Lochinvar!

He stay'd not for brake and he stopt not for stone;
He swam the Eske river where ford there was none;
But ere he alighted at Netherby gate,
The bride had consented; the gallant came late;
For a laggard in love and a dastard in war
Was to wed the fair Ellen of brave Lochinvar.

So bravely he enter'd the Netherby Hall,
Among bridesmen and kinsmen and brothers and all,
Then spake the bride's father, his hand on his sword,
For the poor craven bridegroom said never a word,
'O come ye in peace here, or come ye in war,
Or to dance at our bridal, young Lord Lochinvar?'

'I long woo'd your daughter, my suit you denied;
Love swells like the Solway, but ebbs like its tide;
And now I am come with this lost love of mine
To lead but one measure, drink one cup of wine.
There are maidens in Scotland more lovely by far,
That would gladly be bride to the young Lochinvar!'

The bride kiss'd the goblet, the knight took it up,
He quaff'd off the wine and he threw down the cup;
She look'd down to blush, and she look'd up to sigh,
With a smile on her lips and a tear in her eye.
He took her soft hand ere her mother could bar;
'Now tread we a measure!' said young Lochinvar.

So stately his form, and so lovely her face,
That never a hall such a galliard did grace:
While her mother did fret and her father did fume,
And the bridegroom stood dangling his bonnet and plume;
And the bride-maidens whispered, "Twere better by far
To have match'd our fair cousin with young Lochinvar!'

One touch to her hand and one word in her ear,
When they reach'd the hall door; and the charger stood near;
So light to the croupe the fair lady he swung,
So light to the saddle before her he sprung!
'She is won! we are gone, over bank, bush and scaur,
They'll have fleet steeds that follow!' cried young Lochinvar.

There was mounting 'mong Graemes of the Netherby clan;
Forsters, Fenwicks, and Musgraves, they rode and they ran;
There was racing and chasing on Cannobie lea;
But the lost bride of Netherby ne'er did they see.
So daring in love, and so dauntless in war,
Have ye e'er heard of gallant like young Lochinvar!

Elegia V

In summer's heat, and mid-time of the day,
To rest my limbs upon a bed I lay;
One window shut, the other open stood,
Which gave such light as twinkles in a wood,
Like twilight glimpse at setting of the sun,
Or night being past, and yet not day begun.
Such light to shamefast maidens must be shown,
Where they may sport and seem to be unknown.
Then came Corinna in a long loose gown,
Her white neck hid with tresses hanging down,
Resembling fair Semiramis going to bed,
Or Lais of a thousand wooers sped.
I snatched her gown; being thin, the harm was small,
Yet strived she to be covered therewithal,
And striving thus as one that would be cast,
Betrayed herself, and yielded at the last.
Stark naked as she stood before mine eye,
Not one wen in her body could I spy.
What arms and shoulders did I touch and see,
How apt her breasts were to be pressed by me!
How smooth a belly under her waist saw I,
How large a leg, and what a lusty thigh!
To leave the rest, all liked me passing well;
I clinged her naked body, down she fell.
Judge you the rest: being tired she bade me kiss;
Jove send me more such afternoons as this.

from Ovid's Elegies, *Book I*

The Dirty Talker: D Line, Boston

Shabby, tweedy, academic, he was old enough to be her
  father and I thought he was her father,
then realized he was standing closer than a father would so
  I thought he was her older lover.
And I thought at first that she was laughing, then saw it
  was more serious, more strenuous:
her shoulders spasmed back and forth; he was leaning
  close, his mouth almost against her ear.
He's terminating the affair, I thought: wife ill, the kids . . .
  the girl won't let him go.
We were in a station now, he pulled back half a head from
  her the better to behold her,
then was out the hissing doors, she sobbing wholly now so
  that finally I had to understand –
her tears, his grinning broadly in – at *me* now though, as
  though I were a portion of the story.

A Light Woman

I

So far as our story approaches the end,
  Which do you pity the most of us three?—
My friend, or the mistress of my friend
  With her wanton eyes, or me?

II

My friend was already too good to lose,
  And seemed in the way of improvement yet,
When she crossed his path with her hunting-noose
  And over him drew her net.

III

When I saw him tangled in her toils,
  A shame, said I, if she adds just him
To her nine-and-ninety other spoils,
  The hundredth for a whim!

IV

And before my friend be wholly hers,
  How easy to prove to him, I said,
An eagle's the game her pride prefers,
  Though she snaps at a wren instead!

V

So, I gave her eyes my own eyes to take,
  My hand sought hers as in earnest need,
And round she turned for my noble sake,
  And gave me herself indeed.

The eagle am I, with my fame in the world,
   The wren is he, with his maiden face.
—You look away and your lip is curled?
   Patience, a moment's space!

For see, my friend goes shaking and white;
   He eyes me as the basilisk:
I have turned, it appears, his day to night,
   Eclipsing his sun's disk.

And I did it, he thinks, as a very thief:
   'Though I love her—that, he comprehends—
'One should master one's passions, (love, in chief)
   'And be loyal to one's friends!'

And she,—she lies in my hand as tame
   As a pear late basking over a wall;
Just a touch to try and off it came;
   'T is mine,—can I let it fall?

With no mind to eat it, that's the worst!
   Were it thrown in the road, would the case assist?
'T was quenching a dozen blue-flies' thirst
   When I gave its stalk a twist.

And I,—what I seem to my friend, you see:
   What I soon shall seem to his love, you guess:
What I seem to myself, do you ask of me?
   No hero, I confess.

XII

'T is an awkward thing to play with souls,
　And matter enough to save one's own:
Yet think of my friend, and the burning coals
　He played with for bits of stone!

XIII

One likes to show the truth for the truth;
　That the woman was light is very true:
But suppose she says,—Never mind that youth!
　What wrong have I done to you?

XIV

Well, any how, here the story stays,
　So far at least as I understand;
And, Robert Browning, you writer of plays,
　Here's a subject made to your hand!

ALLEN CURNOW

Dichtung und Wahrheit

A man I know wrote a book about a man he knew
and this man, or so he the man I know said, fucked
and murdered a girl to save her from the others
who would have fucked and murdered this girl
much more painfully and without finer feelings,
for letting the Resistance down and herself be fucked
by officers of the army of occupation, an oblation
sweet-smelling to Mars and equally to porn god Priapus.

What a fucking shame, this man the one the man
I know knew decided, if you want a job done well
do it yourself, and he did and he left her in a bath
of blood from the hole in her neck which he carved
in soldierly fashion, a way we have in the commandos,
after the fuck he knew she didn't of course
was her last, and a far far better thing, wasn't it?
than the bloody fuckup it would have been if he'd left her
to be unzippered and jack-the-rippered by a bunch
of scabby patriots with no regimental pride.

And he had this idea, and he mopped up the mess
and he laid her out naked on a bed with a crucifix
round her neck for those bastards the others
the sods to find, furious it must have made them.
And the man I know who knew this man or some other
man who did never forgot this fucking story,
it wouldn't leave him alone till he'd shown this goon
who actually did or said he did or was said to have done
the fucking deed what a better educated man

would have done and thought in his place.
And he wrote this book.

Experience like that, he exclaimed,
thrown away on a semiliterate whose English
was so imperfect you could hardly be certain
that what he did and what he said were connected,
let alone, by no fault of his own,
ignorant of the literature on the subject.
What can you do, with nothing but a cock
and a knife and a cuntful of cognac,
if you haven't got the talent?

A big one!

'I am that Dido which thou here dost see'

I am that Dido which thou here dost see,
Cunningly framed in beauteous imagery.
Like this I was, but had not such a soul
As Maro feigned, incestuous and foul.
Æneas never with his Trojan host
Beheld my face, or landed on this coast;
But flying proud Iarbas' villainy,
Not moved by furious love or jealousy,
I did with weapons chaste, to save my fame,
Make way for death untimely, ere it came.
This was my end; but first I built a town,
Revenged my husband's death, lived with renown.
Why didst thou stir up Virgil, envious Muse,
Falsely my name and honour to abuse?
Readers, believe historians, not those
Which to the world Jove's thefts and vice expose.
Poets are liars, and for verses' sake
Will make the Gods of human crimes partake.

translated from the Latin of Ausonius

Apollo and Marsyas

The real duel of Apollo
with Marsyas
(absolute ear
versus immense range)
takes place in the evening
when as we already know
the judges
have awarded victory to the god

bound tight to a tree
meticulously stripped of his skin
Marsyas
howls
before the howl reaches his tall ears
he reposes in the shadow of that howl

shaken by a shudder of disgust
Apollo is cleaning his instrument

only seemingly
is the voice of Marsyas
monotonous
and composed of a single vowel
Aaa

in reality
Marsyas relates
the inexhaustible wealth
of his body

bald mountains of liver
white ravines of aliment

rustling forests of lung
sweet hillocks of muscle
joints bile blood and shudders
the wintry wind of bone
over the salt of memory

shaken by a shudder of disgust
Apollo is cleaning his instrument

now to the chorus
is joined the backbone of Marsyas
in principle the same A
only deeper with the addition of rust

this is already beyond the endurance
of the god with nerves of artificial fibre

along a gravel path
hedged with box
the victor departs
wondering
whether out of Marsyas' howling
there will not some day arise
a new kind
of art – let us say – concrete

suddenly
at his feet
falls a petrified nightingale

he looks back
and sees
that the hair of the tree to which Marsyas was fastened
is white
completely

translated from the Polish by Czesław Miłosz

[97]

Cut

For Susan O'Neill Roe

What a thrill—
My thumb instead of an onion.
The top quite gone
Except for a sort of a hinge

Of skin,
A flap like a hat,
Dead white.
Then that red plush.

Little pilgrim,
The Indian's axed your scalp.
Your turkey wattle
Carpet rolls

Straight from the heart.
I step on it,
Clutching my bottle
Of pink fizz.

A celebration, this is.
Out of a gap
A million soldiers run,
Redcoats, every one.

Whose side are they on?
O my
Homunculus, I am ill.
I have taken a pill to kill

The thin
Papery feeling.
Saboteur,
Kamikaze man—

The stain on your
Gauze Ku Klux Klan
Babushka
Darkens and tarnishes and when

The balled
Pulp of your heart
Confronts its small
Mill of silence

How you jump—
Trepanned veteran,
Dirty girl,
Thumb stump.

KEITH DOUGLAS

How to Kill

Under the parabola of a ball,
a child turning into a man,
I looked into the air too long.
The ball fell in my hand, it sang
in the closed fist: *Open Open*
Behold a gift designed to kill.

Now in my dial of glass appears
the soldier who is going to die.
He smiles, and moves about in ways
his mother knows, habits of his.
The wires touch his face: I cry
NOW. Death, like a familiar, hears

and look, has made a man of dust
of a man of flesh. This sorcery
I do. Being damned, I am amused
to see the centre of love diffused
and the waves of love travel into vacancy.
How easy it is to make a ghost.

The weightless mosquito touches
her tiny shadow on the stone,
and with how like, how infinite
a lightness, man and shadow meet.
They fuse. A shadow is a man
when the mosquito death approaches.

Lily Pond

Thinking of new ways to kill you
and bring you back from the dead,
I try drowning you in the lily pond—

holding your head down
until every bubble of breath
is squeezed from your lungs

and the flat leaves and spiky flowers
float over you like a wreath.
I sit on the stones until I'm numb,

until, among reflections of sky,
water-buttercups, spears of iris,
your face rises to the surface—

a face that was always puffy
and pale, so curiously unchanged.
A wind rocks the waxy flowers, curls

the edges of the leaves. Blue dragonflies
appear and vanish like ghosts.
I part the mats of yellow weed

and drag you to the bank, covering
your green algae-stained corpse
with a white sheet. Then, I lift the edge

and climb in underneath—
thumping your chest,
breathing into your mouth.

Porphyria's Lover

The rain set early in to-night,
    The sullen wind was soon awake,
It tore the elm-tops down for spite,
    And did its worse to vex the lake:
    I listened with heart fit to break.
When glided in Porphyria; straight
    She shut the cold out and the storm,
And kneeled and made the cheerless grate
    Blaze up, and all the cottage warm;
    Which done, she rose, and from her form
Withdrew the dripping cloak and shawl,
    And laid her soiled gloves by, untied
Her hat and let the damp hair fall,
    And, last, she sat down by my side
    And called me. When no voice replied,
She put my arm about her waist,
    And made her smooth white shoulder bare,
And all her yellow hair displaced,
    And, stooping, made my cheek lie there,
    And spread, o'er all, her yellow hair,
Murmuring how she loved me—she
    Too weak, for all her heart's endeavour,
To set its struggling passion free
    From pride, and vainer ties dissever,
    And give herself to me for ever.
But passion sometimes would prevail,
    Nor could to-night's gay feast restrain
A sudden thought of one so pale
    For love of her, and all in vain:

So, she was come through wind and rain.
Be sure I looked up at her eyes
    Happy and proud; at last I knew
Porphyria worshipped me; surprise
    Made my heart swell, and still it grew
    While I debated what to do.
That moment she was mine, mine, fair,
    Perfectly pure and good: I found
A thing to do, and all her hair
    In one long yellow string I wound
    Three times her little throat around
And strangled her. No pain felt she;
    I am quite sure she felt no pain.
As a shut bud that holds a bee,
    I warily oped her lids: again
    Laughed the blue eyes without a stain.
And I untightened next the tress
    About her neck; her cheek once more
Blushed bright beneath my burning kiss:
    I propped her head up as before,
    Only, this time my shoulder bore
Her head, which droops upon it still:
    The smiling rosy little head,
So glad it has its utmost will,
    That all it scorned at once is fled,
    And I, its love, am gained instead!
Porphyria's love: she guessed not how
    Her darling one wish would be heard.
And thus we sit together now,
    And all night long we have not stirred,
    And yet God has not said a word!

Orpheus in Soho

His search is desperate!
And the little night-shops of the Underworld
With their kiosks . . . they know it,
The little bars as full of dust as a stale cake,
None of these places would exist without Orpheus
And how well they know it.

. . . when the word goes ahead to the next city,
An underworld is hastily constructed,
With bitch-clubs, with cellars and passages,
So that he can go on searching, desperately!

As the brim of the world is lit,
And breath pours softly over the Earth,
And as Heaven moves ahead to the next city
With deep airs, and with lights and rains,

He plunges into Hades, for his search is desperate!
And there is so little risk . . . down there,
That is the benefit of searching frenziedly
Among the dust-shops and blind-alleys
. . . there is so little risk of finding her
In Europe's old blue Kasbah, and he knows it.

Ode on the Death of a Favourite Cat, Drowned in a Tub of Gold Fishes

'Twas on a lofty vase's side,
Where China's gayest art had dy'd
   The azure flowers, that blow;
Demurest of the tabby kind,
The pensive Selima reclin'd,
   Gazed on the lake below.

Her conscious tail her joy declar'd;
The fair round face, the snowy beard,
   The velvet of her paws,
Her coat, that with the tortoise vies,
Her ears of jet, and emerald eyes,
   She saw; and purr'd applause.

Still had she gaz'd; but 'midst the tide
Two angel forms were seen to glide,
   The Genii of the stream:
Their scaly armour's Tyrian hue
Thro' richest purple to the view
   Betray'd a golden gleam.

The hapless Nymph with wonder saw:
A whisker first and then a claw,
   With many an ardent wish,
She stretch'd in vain to reach the prize.
What female heart can gold despise?
   What Cat's averse to fish?

Presumptuous Maid! with looks intent
Again she stretch'd, again she bent,

Nor knew the gulf between.
(Malignant Fate sat by, and smil'd)
The slipp'ry verge her feet beguil'd,
　　She tumbled headlong in.

Eight times emerging from the flood
She mew'd to ev'ry watry God,
　　Some speedy aid to send.
No Dolphin came, no Nereid stirr'd:
Nor cruel *Tom*, nor *Susan* heard.
　　A Fav'rite has no friend!

From hence, ye Beauties, undeceiv'd,
Know, one false step is ne'er retriev'd,
　　And be with caution bold.
Not all that tempts your wand'ring eyes
And heedless hearts, is lawful prize;
　　Nor all, that glisters, gold.

La Belle Dame sans Merci

O, what can ail thee, knight at arms,
    Alone and palely loitering;
The sedge has withered from the lake,
    And no birds sing.

O, what can ail thee, knight at arms,
    So haggard and so woe-begone?
The squirrel's granary is full,
    And the harvest's done.

I see a lily on thy brow
    With anguish moist and fever-dew,
And on thy cheeks a fading rose
    Fast withereth too.

I met a lady in the meads,
    Full beautiful—a faery's child,
Her hair was long, her foot was light,
    And her eyes were wild.

I made a garland for her head,
    And bracelets too, and fragrant zone,
She looked at me as she did love,
    And made sweet moan.

I set her on my pacing steed
    And nothing else saw all day long;
For sideways would she lean, and sing
    A faery's song.

She found me roots of relish sweet,
    And honey wild and manna dew;

And sure in language strange she said—
    I love thee true.

She took me to her elfin grot,
    And there she gazed and sighed full sore:
And there I shut her wild, wild eyes
    With kisses four.

And there she lullèd me asleep,
    And there I dreamed, ah woe betide,
The latest dream I ever dreamed
    On the cold hill side.

I saw pale kings and princes too,
    Pale warriors, death-pale were they all:
They cry'd—'La belle Dame sans Merci
    Hath thee in thrall!'

I saw their starved lips in the gloam
    With horrid warning gapèd wide,
And I awoke, and found me here
    On the cold hill side.

And this is why I sojourn here
    Alone and palely loitering,
Though the sedge is withered from the lake,
    And no birds sing.

AUGUST KLEINZAHLER

Green Sees Things in Waves

Green first thing each day sees waves –
the chair, armoire, overhead fixtures, you name it,
waves – which, you might say, things really are,
but Green just lies there awhile breathing
long slow breaths, in and out, through his mouth
like he was maybe seasick, until in an hour or so
the waves simmer down and then the trails and colors
off of things, that all quiets down as well and Green
starts to think of washing up, breakfast even
with everything still moving around, colors, trails,
and sounds, from the street and plumbing next door,
vibrating – of course you might say that's what
sound really is, after all, vibrations – but Green,
he's not thinking physics at this stage, nuh-uh,
our boy's only trying to get himself out of bed,
get a grip, but sometimes, and this is the kicker,
another party, shall we say, is in the room
with Green, and Green knows this other party
and they do not get along, which understates it
quite a bit, quite a bit, and Green knows
that this other cat is an hallucination, right,
but these two have a routine that goes way back
and Green starts hollering, throwing stuff
until he's all shook up, whole day gone to hell,
bummer . . .
              Anyhow, the docs are having a look,
see if they can't dream up a cocktail,
but seems our boy ate quite a pile of acid one time,
clinical, wow, enough juice for half a block –

[109]

go go go, little Greenie – blew the wiring out
from behind his headlights and now, no matter what,
can't find the knob to turn off the show.

ALFRED, LORD TENNYSON

Tithonus

The woods decay, the woods decay and fall,
The vapours weep their burthen to the ground,
Man comes and tills the field and lies beneath,
And after many a summer dies the swan.
Me only cruel immortality
Consumes: I wither slowly in thine arms,
Here at the quiet limit of the world,
A white-hair'd shadow roaming like a dream
The ever-silent spaces of the East,
Far-folded mists, and gleaming halls of morn.

 Alas! for this gray shadow, once a man –
So glorious in his beauty and thy choice,
Who madest him thy chosen, that he seem'd
To his great heart none other than a God!
I ask'd thee, 'Give me immortality.'
Then didst thou grant mine asking with a smile,
Like wealthy men who care not how they give.
But thy strong Hours indignant work'd their wills,
And beat me down and marr'd and wasted me,
And tho' they could not end me, left me maim'd
To dwell in presence of immortal youth,
Immortal age beside immortal youth,
And all I was, in ashes. Can thy love,
Thy beauty, make amends, tho' even now,
Close over us, the silver star, thy guide,
Shines in those tremulous eyes that fill with tears
To hear me? Let me go: take back thy gift:
Why should a man desire in any way
To vary from the kindly race of men,

Or pass beyond the goal of ordinance
Where all should pause, as is most meet for all?

A soft air fans the cloud apart; there comes
A glimpse of that dark world where I was born.
Once more the old mysterious glimmer steals
From thy pure brows, and from thy shoulders pure,
And bosom beating with a heart renew'd.
Thy cheek begins to redden thro' the gloom,
Thy sweet eyes brighten slowly close to mine,
Ere yet they blind the stars, and the wild team
Which love thee, yearning for thy yoke, arise,
And shake the darkness from their loosen'd manes,
And beat the twilight into flakes of fire.

Lo! ever thus thou growest beautiful
In silence, then before thine answer given
Departest, and thy tears are on my cheek.

Why wilt thou ever scare me with thy tears,
And make me tremble lest a saying learnt,
In days far-off, on that dark earth, be true?
'The Gods themselves cannot recall their gifts.'

Ay me! ay me! with what another heart
In days far-off, and with what other eyes
I used to watch – if I be he that watch'd –
The lucid outline forming round thee; saw
The dim curls kindle into sunny rings;
Changed with thy mystic change, and felt my blood
Glow with the glow that slowly crimson'd all
Thy presence and thy portals, while I lay,
Mouth, forehead, eyelids, growing dewy-warm
With kisses balmier than half-opening buds
Of April, and could hear the lips that kiss'd

Whispering I knew not what of wild and sweet,
Like that strange song I heard Apollo sing,
While Ilion like a mist rose into towers.

　　Yet hold me not for ever in thine East:
How can my nature longer mix with thine?
Coldly thy rosy shadows bathe me, cold
Are all thy lights, and cold my wrinkled feet
Upon thy glimmering thresholds, when the steam
Floats up from those dim fields about the homes
Of happy men that have the power to die,
And grassy barrows of the happier dead.
Release me, and restore me to the ground;
Thou seest all things, thou wilt see my grave:
Thou wilt renew thy beauty morn by morn;
I earth in earth forget these empty courts,
And thee returning on thy silver wheels.

Sisyphus

Bumpity doun in the corrie gaed whuddran the pitiless
   whun stane.
Sisyphus, pechan and sweitan, disjaskit, forfeuchan and
   broun'd-aff,
sat on the heather a hanlawhile, houpan the Boss didna spy
   him,
seein the terms of his contract includit nae mention of tea-
   breaks,
syne at the muckle big scunnersom boulder he trauchlit
   aince mair.
Ach! how kenspeckle it was, that he ken'd ilka spreckle and
   blotch on't.
Heavin awa at its wecht, he manhaunnlit the bruitt up
   the brae-face,
takkan the easiest gait he had fand in a fudder of dour
   years,
haudan awa frae the craigs had affrichtit him maist in his
   youth-heid,
feelin his years aa the same, he gaed cannily, tenty of
   slipped discs.
Eftir an hour and a quarter he warslit his wey to the brae's
   heid,
hystit his boulder richt up on the tap of the cairn – and it
   stude there!
streikit his length on the chuckie-stanes, houpan the Boss
   wadna spy him,
had a wee look at the scenery, feenisht a pie and a cheese-
   piece.

Whit was he thinkin about, that he jist gied the boulder a
  wee shove?
Bumpity doun in the corrie gaed whuddran the pitiless
  whun stane,
Sisyphus dodderan eftir it, shair of his cheque at the
  month's end.

Leda and the Swan

A sudden blow: the great wings beating still
Above the staggering girl, her thighs caressed
By the dark webs, her nape caught in his bill,
He holds her helpless breast upon his breast.

How can those terrified vague fingers push
The feathered glory from her loosening thighs?
And how can body, laid in that white rush,
But feel the strange heart beating where it lies?

A shudder in the loins engenders there
The broken wall, the burning roof and tower
And Agamemnon dead.
                              Being so caught up,
So mastered by the brute blood of the air,
Did she put on his knowledge with his power
Before the indifferent beak could let her drop?

The Terrorist, He's Watching

The bomb in the bar will explode at thirteen twenty.
Now it's just thirteen sixteen.
There's still time for some to go in,
and some to come out.

The terrorist has already crossed the street.
The distance keeps him out of danger,
and what a view—just like the movies:

A woman in a yellow jacket, she's going in.
A man in dark glasses, he's coming out.
Teenagers in jeans, they're talking.
Thirteen seventeen and four seconds.
The short one, he's lucky, he's getting on a scooter,
but the tall one, he's going in.

Thirteen seventeen and forty seconds.
That girl, she's walking along with a green ribbon in her
    hair.
But then a bus suddenly pulls in front of her.
Thirteen eighteen.
The girl's gone.
Was she that dumb, did she go in or not,
we'll see when they carry them out.

Thirteen nineteen.
Somehow no one's going in.
Another guy, fat, bald, is leaving, though.
Wait a second, looks like he's looking for something in his
    pockets and

at thirteen twenty minus ten seconds
he goes back in for his crummy gloves.

Thirteen twenty exactly.
This waiting, it's taking forever.
Any second now.
No, not yet.
Yes, now.
The bomb, it explodes.

translated from the Polish
by Stanisław Barańczak and Clare Cavanagh

PAUL MULDOON

Meeting the British

We met the British in the dead of winter.
The sky was lavender

and the snow lavender-blue.
I could hear, far below,

the sound of two streams coming together
(both were frozen over)

and, no less strange,
myself calling out in French

across that forest-
clearing. Neither General Jeffrey Amherst

nor Colonel Henry Bouquet
could stomach our willow-tobacco.

As for the unusual
scent when the Colonel shook out his hand-

kerchief: *C'est la lavande,*
une fleur mauve comme le ciel.

They gave us six fishhooks
and two blankets embroidered with smallpox.

RUDYARD KIPLING

Danny Deever

'What are the bugles blowin' for?' said Files-on-Parade.
'To turn you out, to turn you out,' the Colour-Sergeant
  said.
'What makes you look so white, so white?' said Files-on-
  Parade.
'I'm dreadin' what I've got to watch,' the Colour-Sergeant
  said.
> For they're hangin' Danny Deever, you can hear the
>   Dead March play,
> The regiment's in 'ollow square – they're hangin' him
>   to-day;
> They've taken of his buttons off an' cut his stripes
>   away,
> An' they're hangin' Danny Deever in the mornin'.

'What makes the rear-rank breathe so 'ard?' said Files-on-
  Parade.
'It's bitter cold, it's bitter cold,' the Colour-Sergeant said.
'What makes that front-rank man fall down?' said Files-on-
  Parade.
'A touch o' sun, a touch o' sun,' the Colour-Sergeant said.
> They are hangin' Danny Deever, they are marchin' of
>   'im round,
> They 'ave 'alted Danny Deever by 'is coffin on the
>   ground;
> An' 'e'll swing in 'arf a minute for a sneakin' shootin'
>   hound –
> O they're hangin' Danny Deever in the mornin'!

"Is cot was right-'and cot to mine,' said Files-on-Parade.
"E's sleepin' out an' far to-night,' the Colour Sergeant said.
'I've drunk 'is beer a score o' times,' said Files-on-Parade.
"E's drinkin' bitter beer alone,' the Colour-Sergeant said.
    They are hangin' Danny Deever, you must mark 'im to
      'is place,
    For 'e shot a comrade sleepin' – you must look 'im in
      the face;
    Nine 'undred of 'is county an' the regiment's disgrace,
    While they're hangin' Danny Deever in the mornin'.

'What's that so black agin the sun?' said Files-on-Parade.
'It's Danny fightin' 'ard for life,' the Colour-Sergeant said.
'What's that that whimpers over'ead?' said Files-on-Parade.
'It's Danny's soul that's passin' now,' the Colour-Sergeant
  said.
    For they're done with Danny Deever, you can 'ear the
      quickstep play,
    The regiment's in column, an' they're marchin' us away;
    Ho! the young recruits are shakin', an' they'll want
      their beer to-day,
    After hangin' Danny Deever in the mornin'.

The Entertainment of War

I saw the garden where my aunt had died
And her two children and a woman from next door;
It was like a burst pod filled with clay.

A mile away in the night I had heard the bombs
Sing and then burst themselves between cramped houses
With bright soft flashes and sounds like banging doors;

The last of them crushed the four bodies into the ground,
Scattered the shelter, and blasted my uncle's corpse
Over the housetop and into the street beyond.

Now the garden lay stripped and stale; the iron shelter
Spread out its separate petals around a smooth clay saucer,
Small, and so tidy it seemed nobody had ever been there.

When I saw it, the house was blown clean by blast and care:
Relations had already torn out the new fireplaces;
My cousin's pencils lasted me several years.

And in his office notebook that was given me
I found solemn drawings in crayon of blondes without
    dresses.
In his lifetime I had not known him well.

Those were the things I noticed at ten years of age:
Those, and the four hearses outside our house,
The chocolate cakes, and my classmates' half-shocked envy.

But my grandfather went home from the mortuary
And for five years tried to share the noises in his skull,
Then he walked out and lay under a furze-bush to die.

When my father came back from identifying the daughter
He asked us to remind him of her mouth.
We tried. He said 'I think it was the one'.

These were marginal people I had met only rarely
And the end of the whole household meant that no grief
    was seen;
Never have people seemed so absent from their own deaths.

This bloody episode of four whom I could understand better
    dead
Gave me something I needed to keep a long story moving;
I had no pain of it; can find no scar even now.

But had my belief in the fiction not been thus buoyed up
I might, in the sigh and strike of the next night's bombs
Have realised a little what they meant, and for the first time
    been afraid.

As the Team's Head-Brass

As the team's head-brass flashed out on the turn
The lovers disappeared into the wood.
I sat among the boughs of the fallen elm
That strewed the angle of the fallow, and
Watched the plough narrowing a yellow square
Of charlock. Every time the horses turned
Instead of treading me down, the ploughman leaned
Upon the handles to say or ask a word,
About the weather, next about the war.
Scraping the share he faced towards the wood,
And screwed along the furrow till the brass flashed
Once more.
           The blizzard felled the elm whose crest
I sat in, by a woodpecker's round hole,
The ploughman said. 'When will they take it away?'
'When the war's over.' So the talk began—
One minute and an interval of ten,
A minute more and the same interval.
'Have you been out?' 'No.' 'And don't want to, perhaps?'
'If I could only come back again, I should.
I could spare an arm. I shouldn't want to lose
A leg. If I should lose my head, why, so,
I should want nothing more. . . . Have many gone
From here?' 'Yes,' 'Many lost?' 'Yes, a good few.
Only two teams work on the farm this year.
One of my mates is dead. The second day
In France they killed him. It was back in March,
The very night of the blizzard, too. Now if
He had stayed here we should have moved the tree.'

'And I should not have sat here. Everything
Would have been different. For it would have been
Another world.' 'Ay, and a better, though
If we could see all all might seem good.' Then
The lovers came out of the wood again:
The horses started and for the last time
I watched the clods crumble and topple over
After the ploughshare and the stumbling team.

Musée des Beaux Arts

About suffering they were never wrong,
The Old Masters: how well they understood
Its human position; how it takes place
While someone else is eating or opening a window or just
    walking dully along;
How, when the aged are reverently, passionately waiting
For the miraculous birth, there always must be
Children who did not specially want it to happen, skating
On a pond at the edge of the wood:
They never forgot
That even the dreadful martyrdom must run its course
Anyhow in a corner, some untidy spot
Where the dogs go on with their doggy life and the
    torturer's horse
Scratches its innocent behind on a tree.

In Brueghel's *Icarus*, for instance: how everything turns
    away
Quite leisurely from the disaster; the ploughman may
Have heard the splash, the forsaken cry,
But for him it was not an important failure; the sun shone
As it had to on the white legs disappearing into the green
Water; and the expensive delicate ship that must have seen
Something amazing, a boy falling out of the sky,
Had somewhere to get to and sailed calmly on.

Ozymandias

I met a traveller from an antique land
Who said: Two vast and trunkless legs of stone
Stand in the desert . . . Near them, on the sand,
Half sunk, a shattered visage lies, whose frown,
And wrinkled lip, and sneer of cold command,
Tell that its sculptor well those passions read
Which yet survive, stamped on these lifeless things,
The hand that mocked them, and the heart that fed:
And on the pedestal these words appear:
'My name is Ozymandias, king of kings:
Look on my works, ye Mighty, and despair!'
Nothing beside remains. Round the decay
Of that colossal wreck, boundless and bare
The lone and level sands stretch far away.

The Wood-Pile

Out walking in the frozen swamp one grey day,
I paused and said, 'I will turn back from here.
No, I will go on farther—and we shall see.'
The hard snow held me, save where now and then
One foot went through. The view was all in lines
Straight up and down of tall slim trees
Too much alike to mark or name a place by
So as to say for certain I was here
Or somewhere else: I was just far from home.
A small bird flew before me. He was careful
To put a tree between us when he lighted,
And say no word to tell me who he was
Who was so foolish as to think what *he* thought.
He thought that I was after him for a feather—
The white one in his tail; like one who takes
Everything said as personal to himself.
One flight out sideways would have undeceived him.
And then there was a pile of wood for which
I forgot him and let his little fear
Carry him off the way I might have gone,
Without so much as wishing him good-night.
He went behind it to make his last stand.
It was a cord of maple, cut and split
And piled—and measured, four by four by eight.
And not another like it could I see.
No runner tracks in this year's snow looped near it.
And it was older sure than this year's cutting,
Or even last year's or the year's before.
The wood was grey and the bark warping off it

And the pile somewhat sunken. Clematis
Had wound strings round and round it like a bundle.
What held it though on one side was a tree
Still growing, and on one a stake and prop,
These latter about to fall. I thought that only
Someone who lived in turning to fresh tasks
Could so forget his handiwork on which
He spent himself, the labour of his axe,
And leave it there far from a useful fireplace
To warm the frozen swamp as best it could
With the slow smokeless burning of decay.

DEREK MAHON

A Refusal to Mourn

He lived in a small farmhouse
At the edge of a new estate.
The trim gardens crept
To his door, and car engines
Woke him before dawn
On dark winter mornings.

All day there was silence
In the bright house. The clock
Ticked on the kitchen shelf,
Cinders moved in the grate,
And a warm briar gurgled
When the old man talked to himself;

But the doorbell seldom rang
After the milkman went,
And if a coat-hanger
Knocked in an open wardrobe
That was a strange event
To be pondered on for hours

While the wind thrashed about
In the back garden, raking
The roof of the hen-house,
And swept clouds and gulls
Eastwards over the lough
With its flap of tiny sails.

Once a week he would visit
An old shipyard crony,
Inching down to the road
And the blue country bus
To sit and watch sun-dappled
Branches whacking the windows

While the long evening shed
Weak light in his empty house,
On the photographs of his dead
Wife and their six children
And the Missions to Seamen angel
In flight above the bed.

'I'm not long for this world'
Said he on our last evening,
'I'll not last the winter',
And grinned, straining to hear
Whatever reply I made;
And died the following year.

In time the astringent rain
Of those parts will clean
The words from his gravestone
In the crowded cemetery
That overlooks the sea
And his name be mud once again

And his boilers lie like tombs
In the mud of the sea bed
Till the next ice age comes
And the earth he inherited
Is gone like Neanderthal Man
And no records remain.

But the secret bred in the bone
On the dawn strand survives
In other times and lives,
Persisting for the unborn
Like a claw-print in concrete
After the bird has flown.

Napoleon

'What is the world, O soldiers?
    It is I:
I, this incessant snow,
    This northern sky;
Soldiers, this solitude
    Through which we go
        Is I.'

HUBERT WITHEFORD

Ekaterinburg, 16 July 1918

I've lost the power
To move at all

Ridiculously I hear
The shoot at Sandringham
More shots to come

Once I was the Tsar
In pheasant time

There's blood all over here
I feel the line of guns
Aim down at me

Clever Tom Clinch Going to Be Hanged

As clever *Tom Clinch*, while the Rabble was bawling,
Rode stately through *Holbourn*, to die in his Calling;
He stopt at the *George* for a Bottle of Sack,
And promis'd to pay for it when he'd come back.
His Waistcoat and Stockings, and Breeches were white,
His Cap had a new Cherry Ribbon to ty't,
The Maids to the Doors and the Balconies ran,
And said, lack-a-day! he's a proper young Man.
But, as from the Windows the Ladies he spy'd,
Like a Beau in the Box, he bow'd low on each Side;
And when his last Speech the loud Hawkers did cry,
He swore from his Cart, it was a damn'd Lye.
The Hangman for Pardon fell down on his Knee;
Tom gave him a Kick in the Guts for his Fee.
Then said, I must speak to the People a little,
But I'll see you all damn'd before I will *Whittle*.
My Honest Friend *Wild*, may he long hold his Place,
He lengthen'd my Life with a whole Year of Grace.
Take Courage, dear Comrades, and be not afraid,
Nor slip this Occasion to follow your Trade.
My Conscience is clear, and my Spirits are calm,
And thus I go off without Pray'r Book or Psalm.
Then follow the Practice of clever *Tom Clinch*,
Who hung like a Hero, and never would flinch.

MATTHEW SWEENEY

Hanging

Hanging from the lamppost
he could see far—
cars parked to the street's end,
the few late-night walkers
most of whom ignored him
hanging there. He could hear
screams and running feet,
also quick shuffles away
and, eventually, the wah-wahs
that came with blue lights
that led in the dawn.
Then the lights in all the houses
went on, and dressing-gown
wearers gathered, killing yawns.
And flashbulbs exploded,
though he couldn't hold
his head up, and his face
was blue. A megaphone
asked the crowd to go home
as a ladder leant on the lamppost
for someone to ascend.
He looked into this man's eye
as the knife cut him down.

THEODORE ROETHKE

Child on Top of a Greenhouse

The wind billowing out the seat of my britches,
My feet crackling splinters of glass and dried putty,
The half-grown chrysanthemums staring up like accusers,
Up through the streaked glass, flashing with sunlight,
A few white clouds all rushing eastward,
A line of elms plunging and tossing like horses,
And everyone, everyone pointing up and shouting!

On First Looking into Chapman's Homer

Much have I travelled in the realms of gold,
   And many goodly states and kingdoms seen;
   Round many western islands have I been
Which bards in fealty to Apollo hold.
Oft of one wide expanse had I been told
   That deep-browed Homer ruled as his demesne;
   Yet did I never breathe its pure serene
Till I heard Chapman speak out loud and bold:
Then felt I like some watcher of the skies
   When a new planet swims into his ken;
Or like stout Cortez when with eagle eyes
   He stared at the Pacific – and all his men
Looked at each other with a wild surmise –
   Silent, upon a peak in Darien.

Epic

I have lived in important places, times
When great events were decided, who owned
That half a rood of rock, a no-man's land
Surrounded by our pitchfork-armed claims.
I heard the Duffys shouting 'Damn your soul'
And old McCabe stripped to the waist, seen
Step the plot defying blue cast-steel—
'Here is the march along these iron stones'
That was the year of the Munich bother. Which
Was more important? I inclined
To lose my faith in Ballyrush and Gortin
Till Homer's ghost came whispering to my mind
He said: I made the Iliad from such
A local row. Gods make their own importance.

Redemption

Having been tenant long to a rich Lord,
   Not thriving, I resolved to be bold,
   And make a suit unto him, to afford
A new small-rented lease, and cancel th' old.

In heaven at his manor I him sought:
   They told me there, that he was lately gone
   About some land, which he had dearly bought
Long since on earth, to take possession.

I straight return'd, and knowing his great birth,
   Sought him accordingly in great resorts;
   In cities, theatres, gardens, parks, and courts:
At length I heard a ragged noise and mirth

   Of thieves and murderers: there I him espied,
   Who straight, *Your suit is granted*, said, & died.

The Skip

I took my life and threw it on the skip,
Reckoning the next-door neighbours wouldn't mind
If my life hitched a lift to the council tip
With their dry rot and rubble. What you find

With skips is – the whole community joins in.
Old mattresses appear, doors kind of drift
Along with all that won't fit in the bin
And what the bin-men can't be fished to shift.

I threw away my life, and there it lay
And grew quite sodden. 'What a dreadful shame,'
Clucked some old bag and sucked her teeth: 'The way
The young these days . . . no values . . . me, I blame . . .'

But I blamed no one. Quality control
Had loused it up, and that was that. 'Nough said.
I couldn't stick at home, I took a stroll
And passed the skip, and left my life for dead.

Without my life, the beer was just as foul,
The landlord still as filthy as his wife,
The chicken in the basket was an owl,
And no one said: 'Ee, Jim-lad, whur's thee life?'

Well, I got back that night the worse for wear,
But still just capable of single vision;
Looked in the skip; my life – it wasn't there!
Some bugger'd nicked it – *without* my permission.

Okay, so I got angry and began
To shout, and woke the street. Okay. *Okay!*

And I was sick all down the neighbour's van.
And I disgraced myself on the par-*kay*.

And then . . . you know how if you've had a few
You'll wake at dawn, all healthy, like sea breezes,
Raring to go, and thinking: 'Clever you!
You've got away with it.' And then, oh Jesus,

It hits you. Well, that morning, just at six
I woke, got up and looked down at the skip.
There lay my life, still sodden, on the bricks;
There lay my poor old life, arse over tip.

Or was it mine? Still dressed, I went downstairs
And took a long cool look. The truth was dawning.
Someone had just exchanged my life for theirs.
Poor fool, I thought – I should have left a warning.

Some bastard saw my life and thought it nicer
Than what he had. Yet what he'd had seemed fine.
He'd never caught his fingers in the slicer
The way I'd managed in that life of mine.

His life lay glistening in the rain, neglected,
Yet still a decent, an authentic life.
Some people I can think of, I reflected
Would take that thing as soon as you'd say Knife.

It seemed a shame to miss a chance like that.
I brought the life in, dried it by the stove.
It looked so fetching, stretched out on the mat.
I tried it on. It fitted, like a glove.

[142]

And now, when some local bat drops off the twig
And new folk take the house, and pull up floors
And knock down walls and hire some kind of big
Container (say, a skip) for their old doors,

I'll watch it like a hawk, and every day
I'll make at least – oh – half a dozen trips.
I've furnished an existence in that way.
You'd not believe the things you find on skips.

'When that I was and a little tiny boy'

When that I was and a little tiny boy,
   With hey, ho, the wind and the rain;
A foolish thing was but a toy,
   For the rain it raineth every day.

But when I came to man's estate,
   With hey, ho, the wind and the rain;
'Gainst knaves and thieves men shut their gate,
   For the rain it raineth every day.

But when I came, alas, to wive,
   With hey, ho, the wind and the rain;
By swaggering could I never thrive,
   For the rain it raineth every day.

But when I came unto my beds,
   With hey, ho, the wind and the rain;
With toss-pots still had drunken heads,
   For the rain it raineth every day.

A great while ago the world begun,
   With hey, ho, the wind and the rain;
But that's all one, our play is done,
   And we'll strive to please you every day.

WALLACE STEVENS

The Dwarf

Now it is September and the web is woven.
The web is woven and you have to wear it.

The winter is made and you have to bear it,
The winter web, the winter woven, wind and wind,

For all the thoughts of summer that go with it
In the mind, pupa of straw, moppet of rags.

It is the mind that is woven, the mind that was jerked
And tufted in straggling thunder and shattered sun.

It is all that you are, the final dwarf of you,
That is woven and woven and waiting to be worn,

Neither as mask nor as garment but as a being,
Torn from insipid summer, for the mirror of cold,

Sitting beside your lamp, there citron to nibble
And coffee dribble . . . Frost is in the stubble.

The Mower's Song

I

My mind was once the true survey
Of all these meadows fresh and gay,
And in the greenness of the grass
Did see its hopes as in a glass;
When Juliana came, and she
What I do to the grass, does to my thoughts and me.

II

But these, while I with sorrow pine,
Grew more luxuriant still and fine,
That not one blade of grass you spied,
But had a flower on either side;
When Juliana came, and she
What I do to the grass, does to my thoughts and me.

III

Unthankful meadows, could you so
A fellowship so true forgo,
And in your gaudy May-games meet,
While I lay trodden under feet?
When Juliana came, and she
What I do to the grass, does to my thoughts and me.

IV

But what you in compassion ought,
Shall now by my revenge be wrought:
And flow'rs, and grass, and I and all,
Will in one common ruin fall.
For Juliana comes, and she
What I do to the grass, does to my thoughts and me.

And thus, ye meadows, which have been
Companions of my thoughts more green,
Shall now the heraldry become
With which I will adorn my tomb;
For Juliana comes, and she
What I do to the grass, does to my thoughts and me.

To Lizbie Browne

I

Dear Lizbie Browne,
Where are you now?
In sun, in rain?—
Or is your brow
Past joy, past pain,
Dear Lizbie Browne?

II

Sweet Lizbie Browne,
How you could smile,
How you could sing!—
How archly wile
In glance-giving,
Sweet Lizbie Browne!

III

And, Lizbie Browne,
Who else had hair
Bay-red as yours,
Or flesh so fair
Bred out of doors,
Sweet Lizbie Browne?

IV

When, Lizbie Browne,
You had just begun
To be endeared
By stealth to one,
You disappeared,
My Lizbie Browne!

V

Ay, Lizbie Browne,
So swift your life,
And mine so slow,
You were a wife
Ere I could show
Love, Lizbie Browne.

VI

Still, Lizbie Browne,
You won, they said,
The best of men
When you were wed . . .
Where went you then,
O Lizbie Browne?

VII

Dear Lizbie Browne,
I should have thought,
'Girls ripen fast,'
And coaxed and caught
You ere you passed,
Dear Lizbie Browne!

VIII

But, Lizbie Browne,
I let you slip;
Shaped not a sign;
Touched never your lip
With lip of mine,
Lost Lizbie Browne!

IX

So, Lizbie Browne,
When on a day
Men speak of me
As not, you'll say,
'And who was he?'—
Yes, Lizbie Browne!

FERGUS ALLEN

Up and Down

Today I caught sight of the griffon vultures
Making for the land bridge and Africa –
A cue for me to assemble
And drive our sheep, crying and tinkling,
Down from the mile-high summer pastures
To the folds and knives of the valley.

I spend weeks up here on my own
Either side of the longest day,
My mind as empty as an airship.
The dogs run around and do the work
Or flop down on ledges of rock,
Watching for wanderers.

In my country we eat peas with a spoon,
We do not queue for buses, and the demand
For Western diseases of affluence
Far exceeds the supply.
The lammergeiers drop our bones
Out of the blue, hungry for marrow.

Stuck with half-exile and geology,
I have lost the knack of conversation.
Winters in the town are full of awkwardness,
Silence over backgammon
And jokes that pass me by
Screaming like swifts.

Last year in a smoky room I learned
That a fisherman on a visit
Had taken away my girl;

And the old man in the corner,
Curved like a sickle,
Was said to have minded flocks in the mountains.

CARLOS DRUMMOND DE ANDRADE

Quadrille

João loved Teresa who loved Raimundo
who loved Maria who loved Joachim who loved Lili
who loved no one.

João went to the United States, Teresa to a convent,
Raimundo died in an accident, Maria missed her chance,
Joachim killed himself and Lili married J. Pinto Fernandes,
not one of the original cast.

*translated from the Portuguese
by Virginia de Araujo*

Mythology

All my favourite characters have been
Out of all pattern and proportion:
Some living in villas by railways,
Some like Katsimbalis heard but seldom seen,
And others in banks whose sunless hands
Moved like great rats on ledgers.

Tibble, Gondril, Purvis, the Dude of Puke,
Shatterblossom and Duke Bowdler
Who swelled up in Jaffa and became a tree:
Hollis who had wives killed under him like horses
And that man of destiny,

Ramon de Something who gave lectures
From an elephant, founded a society
To protect the inanimate against cruelty.
He gave aslyum to aged chairs in his home,
Lampposts and crockery, everything that
Seemed to him suffering he took in
Without mockery.

The poetry was in the pity. No judgement
Disturbs people like these in their frames
O men of the Marmion class, sons of the free.

MICHAEL HOFMANN

Marvin Gaye

He added the final 'e'
to counteract the imputation of homosexuality.
His father was plain Revd Gay, his son Marvin III.

He slept with his first hooker
in the army, coming off saltpetre.
He thought there was another word for 'virgin' that wasn't
    'eunuch'.

Including duets, he had fifty-five chart entries.
His life followed the rhythm of albums and tours.
He had a 'couple of periods of longevity with a woman'.

He preached sex to the cream suits,
the halter tops and the drug-induced personality disorders.
When his hair receded, he grew a woolly hat and beard.

Success was the mother of eccentricity and withdrawal.
In Ostend he felt the eyes of the Belgians on him,
in Topanga someone cut the throats of his two Great Danes.

At forty-four, back in his parents' house,
any one of a number of Marvins might come downstairs.
A dog collar shot a purple dressing-gown, twice.

Emily Writes Such a Good Letter

Mabel was married last week
So now only Tom left

The doctor didn't like Arthur's cough
I have been in bed since Easter

A touch of the old trouble

I am downstairs today
As I write this
I can hear Arthur roaming overhead

He loves to roam
Thank heavens he has plenty of space to roam in

We have seven bedrooms
And an annexe

Which leaves a flat for the chauffeur and his wife

We have much to be thankful for

The new vicar came yesterday
People say he brings a breath of fresh air

He leaves me cold
I do not think he is a gentleman

Yes, I remember Maurice very well
Fancy getting married at his age
She must be a fool

You knew May had moved?
Since Edward died she has been much alone

It was cancer

No, I know nothing of Maud
I never wish to hear her name again
In my opinion Maud
Is an evil woman

Our char has left
And a good riddance too
Wages are very high in Tonbridge

Write and tell me how you are, dear,
And the girls,
Phoebe and Rose
They must be a great comfort to you
Phoebe and Rose.

Mrs Small

Mrs Small went to the kitchen for her pocketbook
And came back to the living room with a peculiar look
And the coffee pot.
Pocketbook. Pot.
Pot. Pocketbook.

The insurance man was waiting there
With superb and cared-for hair.
His face did not have much time.
He did not glance with sublime
Love upon the little plump tan woman
With the half-open mouth and the half-mad eyes
And the smile half-human
Who stood in the middle of the living-room floor planning
    apple pies
And graciously offering him a steaming coffee pot.
Pocketbook. Pot.

'Oh!' Mrs Small came to her senses,
Peered earnestly through thick lenses,
Jumped terribly. This, too, was a mistake,
Unforgivable no matter how much she had to bake.
For there can be no whiter whiteness than this one:
An insurance man's shirt on its morning run.
This Mrs Small now soiled
With a pair of brown
Spurts (just recently boiled)
Of the 'very best coffee in town.'

'The best coffee in town is what *you* make, Delphine! There
    is none dandier!'
Those were the words of the pleased Jim Small—
Who was no bandier of words at all.
Jim Small was likely to give you a good swat
When he was *not*
Pleased. He was, absolutely, no bandier.

'I don't know where my mind is this morning,'
Said Mrs Small, scorning
Apologies! For there was so much
For which to apologize! Oh such
Mountains of things, she'd never get anything done
If she begged forgiveness for each one.

She paid him.

But apologies and her hurry would not mix.
The six
Daughters were a-yell, a-scramble, in the hall. The four
Sons (horrors) could not be heard any more.

No.
The insurance man would have to glare
Idiotically into her own sterile stare
A moment—then depart,
Leaving her to release her heart
And dizziness

And silence her six
And mix
Her spices and core
And slice her apples, and find her four.
Continuing her part
Of the world's business.

VLADIMIR NABOKOV

A Literary Dinner

Come here, said my hostess, her face making room
for one of those pink introductory smiles
that link, like a valley of fruit trees in bloom,
the slopes of two names.
I want you, she murmured, to eat Dr James.

I was hungry. The Doctor looked good. He had read
the great book of the week and had liked it, he said,
because it was powerful. So I was brought
a generous helping. His mauve-bosomed wife
kept showing me, very politely, I thought,
the tenderest bits with the point of her knife.
I ate—and in Egypt the sunsets were swell;
the Russians were doing remarkably well;
had I met a Prince Poprinsky, whom he had known
in Caparabella, or was it Mentone?
They had traveled extensively, he and his wife;
her hobby was People, his hobby was Life.
All was good and well cooked, but the tastiest part
was his nut-flavored, crisp cerebellum. The heart
resembled a shiny brown date,
and I stowed all the studs on the edge of my plate.

JACQUES PRÉVERT

At the Florist's

A man enters a florist's
and chooses some flowers
the florist wraps up the flowers
the man puts his hand in his pocket
to find the money
the money to pay for the flowers
but at the same time he puts
all of a sudden
his hand on his heart
and he falls

At the same time that he falls
the money rolls on the floor
and then the flowers fall
at the same time as the man
at the same time as the money
and the florist stands there
with the money rolling
with the flowers spoiling
with the man dying
obviously all this is very sad
and she's got to do something
the florist
but she doesn't know quite where to start
she doesn't know
at which end to begin

There's so many things to do
with this man dying
with these flowers spoiling

and this money
this money that rolls
that doesn't stop rolling.

translated from the French
by Lawrence Ferlinghetti

Isidor

Isidor was always plotting
to overthrow the government.
The family lived in one room. . . .
A window rattles,
a woman coughs,
snow drifts over the rooftops . . .
despair. An intelligent household.

One day, there's a knock at the door. . . .
The police! A confusion . . .
Isidor's wife throws herself
on the mattress . . . she groans
as though she is in labor.
The police search everywhere,
and leave. Then a leg comes out . . .
an arm . . . then a head with spectacles.
Isidor was under the mattress!

When I think about my family
I have a feeling of suffocation.
Next time . . . how about the oven?

The mourners are sitting around
weeping and tearing their clothes.
The inspector comes. He looks in the oven . . .
there's Isidor, with his eyes
shut fast . . . his hands are folded.
The inspector nods, and goes.

Then a leg comes out, and the other.
Isidor leaps, he dances . . .

'Praise God, may His Name be exalted!'

Felix Randal

Felix Randal the farrier, O he is dead then? my duty all
    ended,
Who have watched his mould of man, big-boned and
    hardy-handsome
Pining, pining, till time when reason rambled in it and
    some
Fatal four disorders, fleshed there, all contended?

Sickness broke him. Impatient he cursed at first, but
    mended
Being anointed and all; though a heavenlier heart began
    some
Months earlier, since I had our sweet reprieve and ransom
Tendered to him. Ah well, God rest him all road ever he
    offended!

This seeing the sick endears them to us, us too it endears.
My tongue had taught thee comfort, touch had quenched
    thy tears,
Thy tears that touched my heart, child, Felix, poor Felix
    Randal;

How far from then forethought of, all thy more boisterous
    years,
When thou at the random grim forge, powerful amidst
    peers,
Didst fettle for the great grey drayhorse his bright and
    battering sandal!

WILLIAM CARLOS WILLIAMS

The Last Words of My English Grandmother

There were some dirty plates
and a glass of milk
beside her on a small table
near the rank, disheveled bed—

Wrinkled and nearly blind
she lay and snored
rousing with anger in her tones
to cry for food,

Gimme something to eat—
They're starving me—
I'm all right I won't go
to the hospital. No, no, no

Give me something to eat
Let me take you
to the hospital, I said
and after you are well

You can do as you please.
She smiled, Yes
you do what you please first
then I can do what I please—

Oh, oh, oh! she cried
as the ambulance men lifted
her to the stretcher—
Is this what you call

making me comfortable?
By now her mind was clear—

Oh you think you're smart
you young people,

she said, but I'll tell you
you don't know anything.
Then we started.
On the way

we passed a long row
of elms. She looked at them
awhile out of
the ambulance window and said,

What are all those
fuzzy-looking things out there?
Trees? Well, I'm tired
of them and rolled her head away.

ALEKSANDAR RISTOVIĆ

Out in the Open

While crossing a field,
someone who at that moment
is preoccupied with thoughts of suicide
is forced by nature's call
to delay the act,
and so from his squatting position
finds himself taking pleasure
in some blades of grass,
as if seeing them for the first time
from that close,
while his cheeks redden,
and he struggles to pull from his pocket
a piece of paper
with its already composed
farewell note.

translated from the Serbian by Charles Simic

Acknowledgements

The editors and publishers gratefully acknowledge permission to reprint copyright material in this book as follows:

ANNA AKHMATOVA, from *Selected Poems* (Harvill, 1974), copyright © English translation Stanley Kunitz and Max Hayward, 1967, 1968, 1972, 1973, reproduced by permission of the Harvill Press. FERGUS ALLEN, from *Up and Down* (Faber, 1996), reprinted by permission of Faber and Faber Ltd. SIMON ARMITAGE, from *Kid* (Faber, 1992), reprinted by permission of Faber and Faber Ltd. W. H. AUDEN, from *Collected Poems* (Faber, 1976), reprinted by permission of Faber and Faber Ltd. ELIZABETH BISHOP, from *The Complete Poems 1927–1979* (Chatto, 1983), reprinted by permission of Farrar, Straus and Giroux LLC. CHARLES CAUSLEY, from *Collected Poems 1951–1975* (Macmillan, 1975), reprinted by permission of David Higham Associates. ALLEN CURNOW, from *Early Days Yet: New and Collected Poems 1941–1997* (Carcanet, 1997), reprinted by permission of Carcanet Press. CARLOS DRUMMOND DE ANDRADE, from *The Minus Sign* (Carcanet, 1981), reprinted by permission of Carcanet Press. CAROL ANN DUFFY, from *Mean Time* (Anvil, 1993, 1998), reprinted by permission of Anvil Press Poetry Ltd. T. S. ELIOT, from *Collected Poems 1909–1962* (Faber, 1963), reprinted by permission of Faber and Faber Ltd. VICKI FEAVER, from *The Handless Maiden* (Jonathan Cape, 1994), reprinted by permission of The Random House Group Ltd. JAMES FENTON, from *Memory of War and Children in Exile: Poems 1968–1983* (Penguin, 1983), reprinted by permission of Peters Fraser & Dunlop Ltd. ROY FISHER, from *The Dow Low Drop: New and Selected Poems* (Bloodaxe, 1996), reprinted by permission of Bloodaxe Books Ltd. ROBERT FROST, from *The Poetry of Robert Frost* (Jonathan Cape, 1971), reprinted by permission of The Random House Group Ltd. ROBERT GRAVES, from *Complete Poems Volume 1* (Carcanet, 1995), reprinted by permission of Carcanet Press. LAVINIA GREENLAW, from *Night Photograph* (Faber, 1993), reprinted by permission of Faber and Faber Ltd. IAN HAMILTON,

Collected Poems (Faber, 1960), reprinted by permission of Faber and Faber Ltd. PAUL MULDOON, from *Meeting the British* (Faber, 1987), reprinted by permission of Faber and Faber Ltd. VLADIMIR NABOKOV, from *Poems and Problems* (Weidenfeld & Nicholson, 1972), reprinted by permission of the Vladimir Nabokov Estate. DON PATERSON, from *Nil Nil* (Faber, 1993), reprinted by permission of Faber and Faber Ltd. SYLVIA PLATH, from *Collected Poems* (Faber, 1981), reprinted by permission of Faber and Faber Ltd. EZRA POUND, from *Collected Shorter Poems*, reprinted by permission of Faber and Faber Ltd in the UK and Commonwealth, and in Canada reprinted by permission of New Directions Publishing Corp, from Personae, copyright © by Ezra Pound. CRAIG RAINE, 'In the Kalahari Desert', reprinted by permission of David Godwin Associates. OLIVER REYNOLDS, from *The Player Queen's Wife* (Faber, 1987), reprinted by permission of Faber and Faber Ltd. MAURICE RIORDAN, from *A Word from the Loki* (Faber, 1995), reprinted by permission of Faber and Faber Ltd. ALEKSANDAR RISTOVIC, translated Charles Simic, from *Devil's Lunch* (Faber, 1999), reprinted by permission of Faber and Faber Ltd. WALLACE STEVENS, from *Collected poems of Wallace Stevens* (Faber, 1955), copyright © 1942 by Wallace Stevens, reprinted by permission of Faber and Faber Ltd, and in Canada by Alfred A. Knopf, a Division of Random House Inc. MATTHEW SWEENEY, from *Cacti* (Secker & Warburg, 1992), reprinted by permission of the author. WISLAWA SZYMBORSKA, translated by Stanislaw Baranczak and Clare Cavanagh, from *View with a Grain of Sand* (Faber, 1996), reprinted by permission of Faber and Faber Ltd. ROSEMARY TONKS, from *Iliad of Broken Sentences* (Bodley Head, 1967), copyright © Rosemary Tonks 1967, reprinted by permission of Shiel Land Associates. C. K. WILLIAMS, from *Flesh and Blood* (Farrar, Straus and Giroux, 1987), reprinted by permission of Farrar, Straus and Giroux LLC. WILLIAM CARLOS WILLIAMS, from *Collected Poems: 1909–1939, Volume I*, copyright © 1938 by New Directions Publishing Corp., reprinted by permission of New Directions Publishing Corp. HUBERT WITHEFORD, from *A Blue Monkey for a Tomb* (Faber, 1994), reprinted by permission of Faber and Faber Ltd.

Index of Poets

Index of First Lines

[175]